TECHNICAL
REPORT

Analyzing the Operation of Performance-Based Accountability Systems for Public Services

Frank Camm, Brian M. Stecher

EDUCATION

The research described in this report was conducted within RAND Education, a unit of the RAND Corporation, under a grant from a private philanthropic foundation.

Library of Congress Cataloging-in-Publication Data

Camm, Frank A., 1949-
Analyzing the operation of performance-based accountability systems for public services / Frank Camm, Brian M. Stecher.
p. cm.
Includes bibliographical references.
ISBN 978-0-8330-5004-5 (pbk. : alk. paper)
1. Government accountability. 2. Organizational effectiveness. 3. Performance—Management. I. Stecher, Brian M. II. Title.

JF1351.C345 2010
352.6'6—dc22

2010021609

Published 2010 by the RAND Corporation
1776 Main Street, P.O. Box 2138, Santa Monica, CA 90407-2138
1200 South Hayes Street, Arlington, VA 22202-5050
4570 Fifth Avenue, Suite 600, Pittsburgh, PA 15213-2665
RAND URL: http://www.rand.org/
To order RAND documents or to obtain additional information, contact
Distribution Services: Telephone: (310) 451-7002;
Fax: (310) 451-6915; Email: order@rand.org

Preface

This technical report presents an analytic framework for describing how a performance-based accountability system (PBAS) works and uses the framework to identify appropriate questions to ask when studying the operation and impact of PBASs. This document, which introduces a common language that can be used to discuss PBASs and compare research across sectors, should be of interest to researchers and analysts studying performance measurement and accountability.

The framework and the questions introduced here were used by RAND to analyze the development and effects of PBASs in child care, education, health care, public health emergency preparedness (PHEP), and transportation. A separate document directed toward policymakers and agency administrators reports the findings of that analysis, including recommendations for future research on the development and effects of PBASs related to public services (Stecher et al., 2010).

This research has been conducted by RAND Education, a unit of the RAND Corporation, under a grant from a private philanthropic foundation. Questions and comments regarding this research should be directed to Frank Camm at Frank_Camm@rand.org or Brian Stecher at Brian_Stecher@rand.org.

Contents

Figures and Table

Figures

Table

Summary

During the past few decades, governments all over the world have shown interest in collecting information on the performance of the activities that they manage directly or oversee in some capacity and using that information to improve the performance of these activities. Despite broad interest in using performance measurement for management and many initiatives to create such systems, empirical evidence on how well such efforts actually work or where they work best remains limited. This report presents a framework for understanding the creation and operation of one type of management system, which we call a performance-based accountability system (PBAS). We introduce a vocabulary for talking about the structure of a PBAS and its relationships to the delivery of some service. Using this framework, the report identifies a set of questions that can structure an empirical inquiry into the use and impact of PBASs and opportunities to improve their performance.

Definition of a Performance-Based Accountability System

We define a PBAS as a mechanism designed to improve performance by inducing individuals or organizations that it oversees to change their behavior in ways that will improve policy outcomes about which the creators of the PBAS care. To do this, the PBAS (1) identifies specifically whose behavior (individuals or groups of individuals in an organization) it wants to change, (2) tailors an incentive structure to encourage these individuals or organizations to change their behavior, and (3) defines a set of performance measures it can use within the incentive structure to determine whether changes in behavior are promoting the PBAS's goals.

How a Performance-Based Accountability System Changes Service Delivery

After studying PBASs in a variety of sectors, we develop a general framework for describing (1) how a PBAS works in the context of an existing service-delivery activity and (2) what factors affect performance of the PBAS. The framework is organized around four basic sets of relationships that are important to a PBAS:

- the production chain that defines the production relationships relevant to the service of interest
- the traditional government-oversight process that monitors the service-delivery activity of interest in the absence of a PBAS

- the process by which a PBAS is created and updated to motivate enhanced performance in the service-delivery activity of interest
- the government PBAS oversight process that monitors the service-delivery activity following the introduction of a PBAS (and supplements the traditional administrative oversight process).

The fully elaborated framework shows all these elements and describes the connections among them.

Empirical Questions to Ask When Studying a Performance-Based Accountability System

The framework also serves as a useful basis for generating analytic questions about the operation and impact of a PBAS in an area of public service. We identify five basic questions (and related subquestions) to ask about the operation and impact of a PBAS. The basic questions are as follows:

- How did the relevant service-delivery activity work before a PBAS existed?
- Why and how did the PBAS come into existence?
- What does the internal design of the PBAS look like?
- How well does the PBAS work?
- What can be done to enhance our understanding of the PBAS and improve its performance?

These five areas of investigation should help structure future analyses of PBASs, expanding our knowledge of what successful PBASs should look like and helping to identify circumstances in which PBASs are most likely to succeed relative to alternative governance structures.

Acknowledgments

This document is one product of a project in which Cheryl Damberg, Laura Hamilton, Kathleen Mullen, Christopher Nelson, Paul Sorensen, Martin Wachs, Allison Yoh, and Gail Zellman also participated. The arguments presented in this report evolved through the course of the two-year project and benefited repeatedly from regular discussions with these colleagues. Silvia Montoya helped us review recent academic, empirically based literature on the use of performance measurement and performance management in the public sector. Discussions with Kevin Brancato, John Graser, and Mark Lorell in a related RAND project on Air Force performance-based services acquisition influenced our thinking on a number of the arguments developed during our study. Especially careful reviews by RAND colleague Susan Gates and Mark Abramson of Leadership Inc. helped us focus and clarify the primary arguments presented in this report. We also benefited from comments by RAND colleagues Richard Neu and Cathleen Stasz, William Gormley of Georgetown University, and Harry Hatry of the Urban Institute on a closely related product of this project.

We thank them all, but we retain full responsibility for the objectivity, accuracy, and analytic content of the work presented in this report.

Abbreviations

GPRA	Government Performance and Results Act of 1993
NCLB	No Child Left Behind Act of 2001
PBAS	performance-based accountability system
PHEP	public health emergency preparedness
TIMSS	Trends in International Mathematics and Science Study

CHAPTER ONE

Introduction

In the past few decades, private-sector and governmental organizations have become increasingly interested in using formal methods to improve their own performance. In the private sector, quality-based management systems[1] that highlight customer priorities and seek to align production processes to serve those priorities in a more cost-effective manner were initially developed in Japan. They began to spread to American companies in the 1980s, and now they are applied in almost all types of commercial industries and corporate settings through such techniques as lean production and Six Sigma. As interest in privatizing traditionally governmental activities grew in the 1980s, public-sector organizations in a number of English-speaking countries found their own techniques for improving the delivery of public services. Like their commercial counterparts, these techniques increased emphasis on what an activity delivered to its ultimate customer—in this case, members of the general public—and measured the performance of an activity from the outside (focusing on the net value it created) rather than from the inside (focusing on its own priorities). The central ideas behind their approaches have come to be known as new public management. Beginning around 1990, these broad trends hit the United States in a rising tide of local, state, and federal efforts to "reinvent government" that continues to this day. The Government Performance and Results Act of 1993 (Pub. L. 103-62) (GPRA) became the centerpiece of federal efforts to promote performance-based management.[2]

The application of these approaches continues to grow in the public and private sectors, involving ever more organizations and more activities within these organizations. The growing application of formal quality-based management methods in competitive industries strongly suggests that these methods are having a positive effect—how could firms that apply them continue to prosper in competitive settings if these methods were not worth their cost? But what is the evidence that they improve performance in government settings, in which dif-

[1] The glossary provides simple descriptions of the quality-related approaches mentioned in this summary. They share a common theme that production processes, incentive systems, or both must change to increase the cost-effectiveness of activities in achieving an organization's goals.

[2] The activities affected by public-sector initiatives can exist in the public sector, such as in public schools and government-run health facilities. They can also exist in the private sector, as they do in neighborhood child-care centers and for-profit or not-for-profit hospitals. These activities can provide service directly to a government agency, such as a highway construction contractor, or to a private-sector user who pays for at least some portion of the cost of the activity for which public funds partially pay, such as a user of public transit. For descriptions of government agency efforts to improve the performance of the activities they manage or oversee, see Abramson and Kamensky (2001); Brudney, Hebert, and Wright (1999); Burgess and Metcalfe (1999); Ferlie (1998); Kettl (1998); Kettl and DeIulio (1995); Lynn (2006); Moon and deLeon (2001); Moynihan (2006); National Academy of Public Administration and Financial Accounting Foundation (1997); Osborne and Gaebler (1993); Poister and Streib (1999); Radin (2003); Sterck (2007); Thompson (2002); and Wang (2002).

ferent activities occur and very different economic and social factors shape decisionmaking in these activities? In addition, to provide helpful information to public-sector policymakers, researchers would like to know what empirical evidence exists on factors that appear to induce governments to apply these formal methods, which specific methods governments prefer in various situations, how these methods change the organization of and distribution of roles and responsibilities within government activities, and how the methods affect the performance of these government activities.

This report provides an analytic framework for a research study that seeks to answer these questions with respect to one particular method for inducing improvements in governmental activity, a performance-based accountability system, or PBAS. In the simplest form of performance-based management, policymakers monitor the performance of service activities of interest to them and use information on the performance of these activities to improve their provision of services. In what we call a PBAS, policymakers explicitly tie performance measures to incentive structures that they then exploit to promote performance improvements.

For example, in the case in which government controls the delivery of the service, policymakers can directly reward good providers of services and sanction bad providers by tying things about which they care to their realized performance. These incentives might be the income or opportunities of the owners, managers, or employees of organizations that provide services or the budget, authority, or freedom from outside interference of these organizations. For example, a transportation agency can pay a highway contractor more for completing repairs more rapidly. A school district can require schools that perform poorly to make management changes that better-performing schools do not have to make.

Alternatively, in the case in which government is not the provider of the service, policymakers might publicize the identity of high-performing organizations (e.g., child-care providers) to encourage users to seek their services. This approach simultaneously improves the services made available to users by directing them to the best providers and, presumably, rewards the providers with higher demand (as well as the honors, revenues, personal benefits and compensation, and expanded authority that higher demand brings). Publicizing the performance ratings of child-care centers presumably helps match customers to the kinds of providers they seek and helps higher-quality providers justify fees or public support for the higher level of service that they provide.

Policymakers considering the use of PBASs would benefit from answers to a number of questions? How common are PBASs? When and where are they most likely to arise? What do they look like? How well do they work? What lessons can be learned from one PBAS about how to structure another or about how well another might work? Remarkably little formal empirical evidence is available to answer many of these questions.

This report is one product of a research effort to gather readily available empirical information to answer these questions. It presents an analytic framework that we applied to collect and document information on the role, structure, and behavior of PBASs in five sectors: child care, education, health care, public health emergency preparedness (PHEP), and transportation. Chapter Two presents our understanding of the key elements of a PBAS and the factors that are relevant to how the PBAS works. Chapter Three uses the material in Chapter Two to identify more specific and focused questions that helped us organize the empirical information we collected on PBASs in the five sectors. The questions focus inquiry on why these PBASs appeared where they did, why they look the way they do, how they work, and how well they work. Chapter Four briefly recaps the material discussed here, and an appendix summarizes the key elements of a PBAS in one table.

A companion monograph (Stecher et al., 2010) presents the results of our analysis of PBASs in these five sectors. It explains what PBASs look like in each of these sectors, focusing mainly on experience in the United States. It then looks across these five sectors, using information from each sector to identify insights that hold across the sectors. These insights clarify the role, design, behavior, and performance of PBASs; suggest ways to improve their design and performance; and point to areas in which additional formal empirical analysis could expand our understanding of the role, design, behavior, and, ultimately, the performance of PBASs as a management tool available to government policymakers.

CHAPTER TWO

How a Performance-Based Accounting System Changes Service Delivery: An Analytic Overview

This chapter describes a simple analytic framework that provides a common vocabulary that can be used to analyze (1) how a PBAS works in the context of an existing service-delivery activity and (2) what factors affect performance of the PBAS. The framework is organized around four basic sets of relationships that are important to a PBAS:

- the production chain that defines the production relationships relevant to the service of interest
- the traditional government-oversight process that monitors the service-delivery activity of interest in the absence of a PBAS
- the process by which a PBAS is created and updated to motivate enhanced performance in the service-delivery activity of interest
- the government PBAS oversight process that monitors the service-delivery activity following the introduction of a PBAS (and supplements the traditional administrative oversight process).[1]

This chapter describes each of these sets of relationships in turn and then shows how they all relate to one other. The appendix inventories the key elements and relationships discussed here in a single table.

The Production Chain

In our framework, a *service-delivery activity* transforms *inputs* into *outputs*. In principle, it is feasible to observe inputs going directly into the activity and outputs coming directly out of it. The outputs are valued because they ultimately lead to outcomes about which policymakers, taxpayers, and citizens care.[2] A *production chain* defines prevailing beliefs about the end-to-end

[1] Nongovernmental activities sustain some PBASs that we examine in the health-care policy domain. This framework treats them as though they are acting in a governmental capacity. The framework accommodates such nongovernmental activities without difficulty, but we must keep in mind that they operate in very different environments from governmental sponsors of PBASs, facing different opportunities and constraints. The discussion in this chapter attempts to highlight such differences when they appear to be important.

[2] Such a structure might be called a production function in the economic literature, a process map in the engineering literature, or a logic model in the program-evaluation literature. An economic production function explains how a process transforms one set of goods or services into another. A logic model is a plausible and sensible model of how a program will work under certain environmental conditions. The constituent elements of a logic model are resources, activities, outputs, and short-, intermediate-, and longer-term outcomes. Some users add, as we do here, customers served and relevant external

set of processes and relationships that transform inputs into outputs and then translates outputs and their production into outcomes. Figure 2.1 displays such a chain. *Inputs* (box IN)[3] include variable resources, such as money, material inputs, contract labor, leased assets, and perishable information, and the services of fixed assets, such as buildings, equipment, information systems, long-term employees, and concepts of operations.

A *service-delivery activity* (box SD) combines such inputs to produce *outputs*. Service-delivery activities include such things as delivering education, providing health care, offering child care, and developing and maintaining infrastructure; service-delivery activities also include the provision of information relevant to public or private activities; the creation of such capabilities as emergency preparedness; and investment activities, such as research and development or construction of public housing. For our analysis, we define outputs to be products that we can clearly associate with a service-delivery activity. For example, we can observe numbers of graduates, vaccinated children, repaired roads, or people trained for emergency response (box OP).

Citizens, taxpayers, and policymakers are usually more interested in long-term *outcomes* (box OC) that might ultimately result from an activity than in its specific outputs. For example, the public desires educated adults with useful skills and a sense of civic and personal responsibility; test scores and graduation rates are indicators of progress toward this goal. Similarly, child-vaccination rates provide one indication that we might be raising the quality of health in the population as a whole. The public desires a functioning transportation grid that gets people where they want to go cost-effectively, and one step toward that outcome is having

Figure 2.1
The Production Chain That Delivers Services

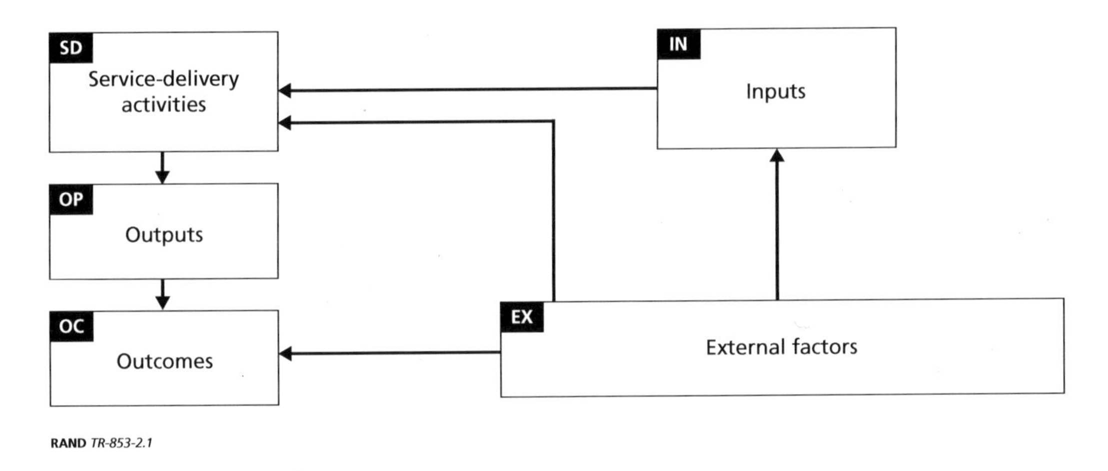

contextual influences. A logic model helps translate findings from evaluation and measurement into a performance story. In our setting, this story has direct and immediate implications for a service-delivery activity in the form of rewards and sanctions, discussed later in this chapter. In addition, the process of developing the logic model can help bring people together within an organization to build a shared understanding of the program and program performance. Internally, it can help program staff gain a common understanding of how the program works and their responsibilities to make it work. It can also help to communicate information about the program to parties outside. Recent articles on logic modeling, with useful references, include Gasper (2000) and McLaughlin and Jordan (2004).

[3] The letters on the boxes on Figures 2.1 through 2.4 are chosen to correspond to the boxes in Figure 2.5, which brings them all together as parts of one system. The letters in themselves have no significance; they are chosen to capture the implicit sequence of events that occur when all elements of the system work together.

roads that are kept properly repaired. Having people trained to respond to emergencies is less important than effective response when emergencies occur. By definition, we distinguish outputs from outcomes in the following way. We can easily link outputs to a service-delivery activity. We can easily link outcomes to things about which citizens, taxpayers, and policymakers care. Although this distinction is clear in theory, a bright line rarely distinguishes these two concepts. However, because these two concepts are important to our analysis in different ways, we draw a clear distinction.[4]

It is common for the observable outputs that we value (because we believe that they ultimately lead to valuable outcomes) also to be accompanied by *unintended consequences* (also included in box OP). Vaccinations that protect most children might unavoidably injure a small fraction of those vaccinated. Road repairs inevitably create traffic disruptions while they occur. Emergency training in public spaces can create anxiety that does not prepare the general public well for real emergencies. Thus, unintended consequences are also products of service-delivery activities. Unintended consequences can occur as outcomes, as well. For example, overprescription of antibiotics—a current health-care output—can promote the development of bacteria resistant to these antibiotics and reduce the health status in the future of populations that might have used this antibiotic—a future health-care outcome.

Finally, there are factors external to the process that influence it but are beyond the control of any actor in the production chain (box EX). These external factors can affect inputs, service delivery, and outcomes. For example, unexpected budget shortfalls can limit the resources available to pay for inputs to any activity. Steel might be required to build bridges, but its availability might fall or its cost might increase because of economic activities on the other side of the world. A drug critical to the treatment of patients during an epidemic might unexpectedly become unavailable because a failure in the one plant that produces this drug suddenly leads to the decertification of that plant as a source. Similarly, a shift in the demographics of a user population in a particular area can change the effectiveness of education or child-care services delivered there. For example, an increase in the proportion of families with limited English proficiency can increase the need for basic literacy services as part of child care or education.

External factors can also affect the relationship between outputs and outcomes (box OC). For example, effective response to emergencies depends on having the right response capacity in the right location. If tornadoes and hurricanes occur at unexpected times or in unexpected places, responsiveness will fall, even if traditional preparation appeared to be excellent. A bit more subtly, an unexpectedly deep recession can reduce the employment rate and access to higher education for recent high-school graduates, no matter how well they were educated in high school.

Figure 2.1 captures all such effects as *external factors* that are beyond the control of the service-delivery activity itself.[5]

---

[4] This distinction departs somewhat from that which many evaluation specialists use when building logic models. They often refer to the things we call *outputs* as *intermediate outcomes* so that evaluators can give service activities credit for positively affecting outcomes that the activities are confident they can affect and for which they are comfortable about being held accountable. For example, see Hatry (1999) and McLaughlin and Jordan (2004). Because we focus so directly on incentivizing performance measures, we want to highlight the distinction between measures of things that service activities comfortably affect—in our parlance, *outputs* that we can observe, measure, and link confidently to the specific service activities that produce them—and *outcomes*, which we cannot link confidently to specific service activities but which are the performance entities that really interest policymakers.

[5] Figure 2.1 does not show where the government fits in the production chain. That will become apparent later.

Operating a Service-Delivery Activity Under Traditional Government Administrative Oversight

The discussion of the production chain in Figure 2.1 omits any human actors. Real service-delivery activities involve human decisionmakers at every stage in the production chain. In the public-service areas we are studying, government administrative oversight attempts to influence these human actors to produce the desired outputs and outcomes, whether the service-delivery activities in question are operated inside or outside the government.[6] If an activity operates inside the government, governmental administrative oversight can apply all the tools of governance available within a public-sector hierarchy. If the activity operates outside the government, government administrative oversight is constrained to arm's-length tools, such as contracts, regulation, and taxation.[7] Figure 2.2 offers a simplified depiction of how either approach to influencing the service activity occurs under traditional government oversight.

The government agency that oversees the service-delivery activity has an explicit or implicit set of goals (box GO). These goals help administrators develop and execute a plan for oversight, which they execute during some cycle—for example, a budget year (box TO). Of course, neither plans nor execution is error free, both because of human failures and because of external factors. The same set of external factors discussed in the production chain operates

Figure 2.2
Operating a Service-Delivery Activity Under Traditional Government Oversight

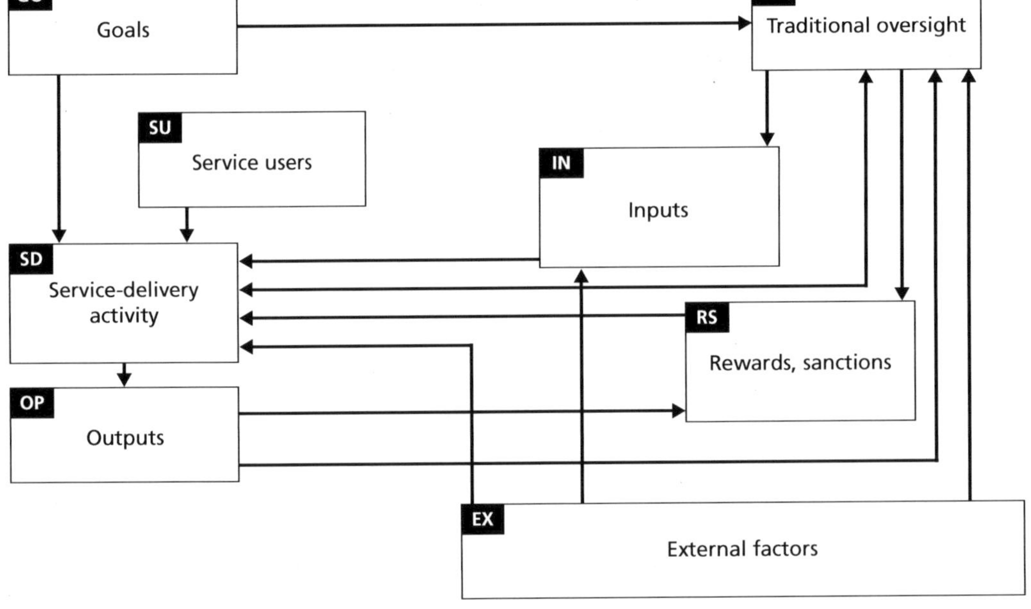

RAND *TR-853-2.2*

[6] These human decisionmakers, of course, are present and influential in the production chain whether or not the government has any particular interest in the chain. We focus on circumstances in which the government does have an interest and uses a PBAS to affect the behavior of these decisionmakers.

[7] A more detailed discussion continues later in this chapter.

here (box EX). For example, changes in government priorities elsewhere might lead oversight officials here to change their planned distribution of funds to various service-delivery activities.

The government administrative oversight agency can deliver two things to the service-delivery activity: the inputs needed to operate and a set of arrangements to motivate the service-delivery activity to operate as the government agency wants it to. These arrangements can include tangible and precise rules and regulations, such as requirements regarding safety, acquisition, hiring, environmental performance, and production quotas. It can include professional standards and codes of ethics. It can include standard operating procedures and time-worn official truisms that hardly register in people's minds, even as they shape behavior. It can include charismatic leadership and moral suasion. Where an administrative oversight system is loosely coupled, as in education, these channels of influence can be quite diffuse, allowing considerable autonomy. Even where the oversight system is tighter, as in highway construction contracting, there is still a fair amount of autonomy with respect to the process of service delivery. In addition to any direct motivational input that might come from the oversight agency, the government's goals might in themselves command the respect of decisionmakers within the service-delivery activity and so influence them via moral suasion (via arrow GO->SD). Staff in the service-delivery activity act on the guidance they have received and use it to decide how to transform the inputs into outputs (box SD).

Government administrative overseers monitor ongoing performance in the service-delivery activity, including the outputs produced (arrows TO<-->SD and OP->TO). If service delivery occurs as planned over the cycle of oversight, they might do little to deviate from the plan. If service delivery does not meet expectations (either because external factors intervene or because behavior within the service-delivery activity differs from what is needed to produce desired outputs), the administrative overseers might change the flow of resources to the activity (arrow TO->IN). They might withdraw resources if the resources are needed more elsewhere: They might add resources to cover a shortfall in service delivery. They might provide technical assistance to correct failures in service delivery. Or they might invest to correct unexpected equipment failures or to exploit unanticipated opportunities. In sum, during the cycle of oversight, administrative overseers can interact actively with the service-delivery activity.

In addition to these administrative relationships, the users of the service being delivered express their preferences about service—either directly in terms of demand for the service or indirectly in terms of public expressions about it, suggestions for changes, or other feedback (box SU). Depending on the incentives that they perceive, staff in the service-delivery activity can react to the input from users in many ways. For example, if the service-delivery activity is a profit center and its revenues flow primarily from sales to users, the activity is likely to be quite responsive to expressed user demand. If the activity receives revenues that do not depend on user demand, it might be less responsive.

At the end of the cycle of oversight, the administrative overseers compile their observations related to boxes SD and OP. The observations might relate to how the service-delivery activity ran during the period and to outputs and unintended consequences. The former might include observations about efficiency, compliance with safety or environmental regulations, appropriate maintenance of long-lived assets, completion of mandatory training, or simply the level of effort of personnel in the activity.

The administrative overseers use the information they have compiled as a basis for rewards or sanctions for the individuals or organizations associated with the service-delivery activity (box RS). In traditional oversight, rewards and sanctions can take the form of changes in budget or other inputs to the activity, changes in roles and responsibilities of the provider organization, or changes in monetary compensation, responsibilities, access to training, and so on for individuals (arrow TO->RS). Presumably, the rewards or sanctions affect the behavior of the organizations and individuals in the service delivery in the next oversight cycles (arrow RS->SD).

Creating and Updating a Performance-Based Accountability System

If policymakers are not content with outputs or outcomes achieved using traditional oversight (Figure 2.3), they might choose to adopt a PBAS to give greater emphasis to quantity, quality, or cost of outputs when determining rewards and sanctions; to link rewards and sanctions more explicitly to measured performance; or to increase the discretion of staff in service-delivery activities in exchange for increased emphasis on results.[8] The *policymakers* who create a PBAS can exist at different administrative levels for different kinds of PBASs (box PM). They might be members of Congress concerned about how to allocate federal resources to state and local emergency preparedness activities. Or they might be high-level bureaucrats in a city agency responsible for the maintenance of subway stations. The only requirement is that they have the authority to set high-level policy goals and to create rules and regulations that influence the activity. As they create the rules and regulations of a PBAS, political pressures, their own altruistic impulses, or their own self-interests can potentially shape their decisions.

Figure 2.3 illustrates how such policymakers create or update a PBAS. The policymakers consider inputs of three kinds as they proceed: information from constituents, information about how the service-delivery activity of interest operates, and information on the quantity, quality, or cost of outputs that the activity generates.

Information from Constituents

Our review of PBAS formation in five sectors suggests that PBASs often originate as part of a political process that raises concerns relevant to the service-delivery activity in question. This process is likely to continue to shape high-level policy relevant to the PBAS as the PBAS operates. A wide range of constituents might be relevant. We highlight two groups: (1) individuals and organizations that *use the outputs* of the service-delivery activity (box SU) and (2) individuals and organizations that directly or indirectly *provide* the service-delivery activity itself (box SD).[9] For example, drivers heavily dependent on a highway experiencing heavy repairs might complain about traffic delays to their city government. Administrators might respond by using a PBAS to speed construction work on the highway. Companies with experience speeding construction work—e.g., working through the night, coordinating inspections, aligning

---

[8] Policymakers might adopt a PBAS for other reasons—for example, because someone else requires them to or because adopting a PBAS gives them some intrinsic value, such as feeling like they are part of a broader movement that they value for some reason. The model offered here provides a nominal baseline that, at least in principle, supports empirical testing to detect such alternative motivations if they are present.

[9] Other constituents might well play important roles. For example, citizens seeking "better government" might advocate the use of PBASs. As important as such constituents might be, parties closer to an activity directly affected by a PBAS have a greater stake in how the PBASs are designed and operated. We expect them to play the largest roles in the initial design and ongoing updating of these oversight mechanisms. If evidence becomes available to reject this expectation, we will adjust the framework.

Figure 2.3
Creating and Updating a Performance-Based Accountability System

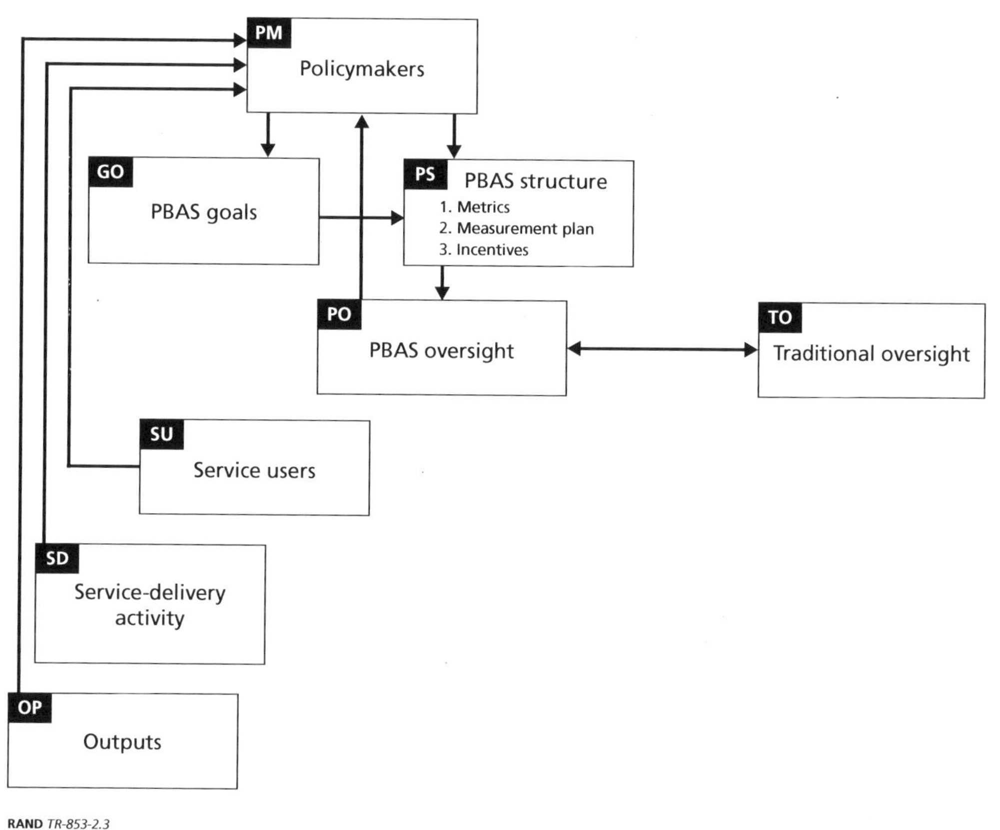

RAND *TR-853-2.3*

suppliers—might petition a city government to use a PBAS so that they will be more likely to win any competition. Users of child care might petition their legislators to implement a PBAS that requires all child-care providers to provide certain information in a standard form that the users can then use to choose among providers. High-quality providers of child care might petition their legislators to have government programs that pay for child care adopt PBASs that pay more for higher-quality child care.

Information About How the Service-Delivery Activity of Interest Operates

Information in box SD would initially come from standard administrative information systems or special evaluations. In education, for example, this might involve class sizes, certification levels for teachers in various subjects, levels of satisfaction among staff, conditions of school infrastructure, or availability of computers. Once a PBAS is in place, it could generate additional information that policymakers can use to modify the PBAS in the future.

Information on the Quantity, Quality, or Cost of Outputs That the Activity Delivers

Again, information in box OP would initially come from standard administrative information systems or special evaluations. Stand-alone evaluations could provide information on intended and unintended consequences. In education, the information might include test scores, such as Regents Examinations or tests prescribed to implement the No Child Left Behind Act of 2001 (Pub. L. 107-110) (NCLB); the number of graduates or graduation rates in different programs (e.g., college-bound or vocational); the number of students with special awards, such as National Merit Scholarships; or the number of students going on to college. The information might be broken down in terms of the demographic characteristics of students, such as race, gender, or home location. Again, a PBAS can also provide supplemental information for future review. Policymakers collect information from these sources, weigh options, and ultimately choose policies, which might include a PBAS.

When they create a PBAS, we expect policymakers to do at least two things. First, they identify *high-level outcome goals* relevant to the service-delivery activity (box GO). Initially, they are likely to endorse broad goals reflecting the kinds of outputs they would like the system to support in the future. At some point, policymakers need to develop proximate performance measures that they can tie more directly to the activities overseen by the PBAS. Despite the preferences of some policymakers for operating at the level of outcomes, the PBAS will not be able to measure outcomes until well after the fact, and, even then, many external factors can affect how the outputs of a service-delivery activity are ultimately transformed into outcomes. Often, agency heads or administrative staff play a role in specifying specific measurable results. For example, a transportation department might highlight average commute times on major arteries during rush hours. An office overseeing education might highlight the percentage of high-school graduates who are gainfully employed or continuing their education six months following graduation. An office overseeing health care might highlight the level of satisfaction of patients treated in hospitals a year following their treatment.

Second, policymakers create a structure for the operation of the PBAS (box PS). The PBAS structure defines the rules and guidelines that will apply during each period of accountability. During a period of accountability, PBAS administrative overseers apply the rules and guidelines to link the activity's performance to specific rewards and sanctions defined by the PBAS structure.[10] The arrow GO->PS shows that the goals can potentially frame the plan and, in particular, the specific types of metrics chosen to measure performance in the plan.[11]

The PBAS structure includes four kinds of rules and guidelines. First, the structure defines what information the PBAS will collect on the performance of the service-delivery activity. It defines this information in terms of specific performance metrics (box PS.1). A performance metric captures an element of performance that can, in principle, be monitored using a qualitative or quantitative measure. For example, a relevant metric might be the change in commute times on urban freeways during the period of accountability.

---

[10] We distinguish a period of accountability under a PBAS from the cycle relevant to traditional oversight to allow for the possibility that the PBAS period of accountability is different from the traditional cycle. For example, in the U.S. federal government, traditional oversight operates in the context of a complex fiscal system that treats a fiscal year—the period of October one year through September in the next year—as the operational cycle relevant to oversight. Resources are programmed and budgeted for such a fiscal year, executed through the course of that year and, in principle, evaluated afterward to determine whether the resources yielded what was expected. A federal PBAS might operate on the same cycle. Or it could use a three-month or four-month period of accountability instead. Whatever the cycles and periods of accountability are under traditional and PBAS oversight, effective oversight under a PBAS will benefit from effective integration of the two.

[11] Suppose a nongovernmental activity creates a PBAS to generate a scorecard. In this case, the leaders of this activity play the role of policymakers (box PM). They collect inputs from their constituents (potentially, boxes SU and SD) and their information sources on service providers (box SD) and service outputs (box OP). They draw up their own goals (box GO) and plan for the structure of a PBAS (box PS). As they define the structure of the PBAS, they cannot directly change any government policies or practices (box PS), but they are likely to consider how they want their PBAS to interact with ongoing government activities (box TO) that affect the service-delivery activity of interest.

Second, the PBAS defines a way to collect information on this metric (box PS.2). It defines one or more *measures*—quantitative or qualitative variables that the PBAS can use to track performance on any metric of interest or against any target of interest. An appropriate measure for urban commute time might be the median commute time in the city during a diurnal period corrected for predictable seasonal effects and other factors, such as scheduled construction. It then defines a *method of measurement* that defines how the PBAS will collect and refine data on any measure and how the PBAS will ensure the integrity of these data. The method of measurement for median commute time might be a formal monthly survey of 1,000 persons who commuted during the diurnal period for the entire previous month.

Third, the PBAS structure includes a process for transforming the values collected on performance metrics into appropriate rewards or sanctions associated with performance during the period of accountability. This process defines the *incentive structure* for the PBAS (box PS.3).[12] Such a structure can define rewards and sanctions for organizations or individuals. For example, it might expand the budget or roles and responsibilities of an organization that performs well as a service-delivery activity. Or, if the organization primarily sells its services to private users, the structure might reward good performance by publicizing information on that performance and thereby increasing demand for the organization's output. Alternatively, it might reward key staff in that activity with bonuses, promotions, new job or training opportunities, or special awards of recognition.

Finally, the PBAS has its own oversight structure (box PO), which assigns the rewards and sanctions. The process defined by the incentive structure might apply detailed, fixed formulas to choose appropriate rewards or sanctions. Or it might leave a great deal of discretion in the hands of PBAS administrative overseers to choose rewards or sanctions that they believe, in their subjective judgment, are appropriate.

The PBAS oversight structure must contend with the traditional administrative oversight structure (arrow PO<->TO). One goal would be to *adjust elements of the administrative oversight and incentive structure* in place before the PBAS was introduced to ensure that the PBAS is effectively integrated with traditional government oversight of the service-delivery activity. For example, it might be important to adjust the mechanisms used in the past to choose budgets and roles and responsibilities for organizations and raises, promotions, training opportunities, and so on for individuals. Somehow, it must coordinate resource flows relevant to the PBAS with resource flows that previously provided funds, personnel, and so on for the service-delivery activity.

As part of the process of implementing a PBAS, policymakers might choose to train individuals on how to apply a PBAS and how to respond to one when it is applied. They might choose to use a communication plan to encourage individuals and organizations to apply and respond to the PBAS properly. Someone has to pay for such supporting activities. More broadly, the effects of a PBAS depend heavily on the degree to which the roles and responsibilities within that activity are expanded to give staff greater authority to shape the activity. This can occur only if traditional roles and responsibilities change. And a government agency might

---

[12] Like van Helden and Tillema (2005), we distinguish measures of performance, captured by the performance metrics described earlier, from incentive structures, which describe the channels through which changes in performance metrics affect the immediate well-being of specific individuals and activities within an organization, which we characterize as rewards and sanctions. A PBAS must have both to improve behavior within any specific institutional setting.

introduce a PBAS as part of a broader plan to add technical assistance and new equipment or production processes for a service-delivery activity.

The effects of a PBAS ultimately depend on how well the government coordinates all of the changes in box PS with traditional administrative activities that the government continues to use to oversee the service-delivery activity in question (box TO). Even with no changes in standard administrative systems, new metrics and incentives could easily disrupt government oversight of a service-delivery activity. Coordination is a challenge for any PBAS and more challenging as the PBAS changes the basic mechanisms employed in traditional administrative oversight. As more mechanisms change, the potential for competing mechanisms to work at cross-purposes rises.

We expect the degree of detail in the plan that defines the structure of a PBAS to differ from one PBAS to the next. For example, it seems reasonable to expect a plan to be refined within a hierarchical planning activity, becoming increasingly detailed as it moves to lower levels, closer to the relevant service-delivery activities. This might occur, for example, as a PBAS plan was defined at a federal, then a state, and finally a city or county level. And it seems reasonable to expect that, at lower levels in a hierarchical plan, some versions of the plan will be more detailed than others. We expect the degree of detail to grow dramatically as we move from the high-level structure that such a hierarchy creates for a PBAS to the operation of that structure over a period of accountability, which we discuss in the next section.

Policymakers are also the ones who update or revise a PBAS over time. Policymakers can observe what results from the application of the PBAS and can adjust the PBAS over time in response. They can use a broad range of formal or informal mechanisms to close the loop between realized performance and the structure of the PBAS that affects this performance. Once a PBAS is in place, such feedback can occur when information flows, by whatever means, upward to policymakers from the PBAS oversight activity (box PO), the service-delivery activity (box SD), and its outputs and unintended consequences (box OP). For example, a PBAS could monitor and report on the hours served by doctors in training, allowing policymakers to ask whether the PBAS needs to address the number of hours. It can monitor and report on the utilization rates for facilities and numbers of serious infections contracted by patients during in-patient care. It can monitor and report on the number of patients served by various departments of the hospital and satisfaction rates for those patients.[13] It can monitor how much it costs to run the PBAS itself. A closed-loop oversight mechanism helps the policymakers ensure that the PBAS is not encouraging behavior in the service-delivery activity that was not intended and is yielding the outputs that were intended. It can also give the policymakers information that they can use to address petitions from interested constituents—to verify that their requests are compatible with the facts available about the service-delivery activity and its outputs and to document benefits from the PBAS relevant to these constituents.[14]

---

[13] Figure 2.3 expresses these feedbacks as information flows directly from the service-delivery activity to policymakers, along arrows SD->PM and OP->PM. These would flow, of course through channels within the PBAS once it was in place. For simplicity, we do not show such detail in Figure 2.3. Our intent here is to highlight the access policymakers have to information on ongoing operations associated with the service-delivery activity.

[14] Note that, in Figure 2.2, we can interpret policymakers as transforming inputs from constituents, a service-delivery activity, and its outputs and unintended consequences into a set of high-level outcome goals and a concrete PBAS plan. That is, the logic map in Figure 2.2 is completely analogous to that in Figure 2.1. Only the transformation activity, and the inputs and outputs associated with it, differ.

Operating a Performance-Based Accountability System During a Period of Accountability

With a PBAS structure in hand, the government can now oversee a service-delivery activity in a different way. Figure 2.4 builds on Figure 2.2 by adding the PBAS and adjusting other boxes to reflect how responsibilities and actions in these boxes are likely to change in the presence of a PBAS.

The introduction of a PBAS changes the relative importance assigned to traditional goals and PBAS-specific outcome goals. Under traditional arrangements, service-delivery agencies can often focus on the outputs they think are most important and pay less attention to the broader goals. In such a traditional environment, the formal goals can come to serve a rhetorical role, much like that in the preamble of a regulation or law. They express high-level values without explaining how they will affect real decisions. A PBAS seeks to take any statement of goals out of the preamble and integrate it fully into the operational language of oversight. It also seeks to make any statement of goals more outcome-oriented, moving an agency to view itself as a vehicle for pursuing goals outside and beyond itself. Making goals both more operationally meaningful and more outcome-oriented requires a careful balancing act.

As noted previously, goals influence the design of the structure of a PBAS (arrow GO->PS)—i.e., the rules and guidelines applied by PBAS administrative overseers during the subsequent period of accountability. To the extent that the goals of the offices with

Figure 2.4
Operating a Performance-Based Accountability System During a Period of Accountability

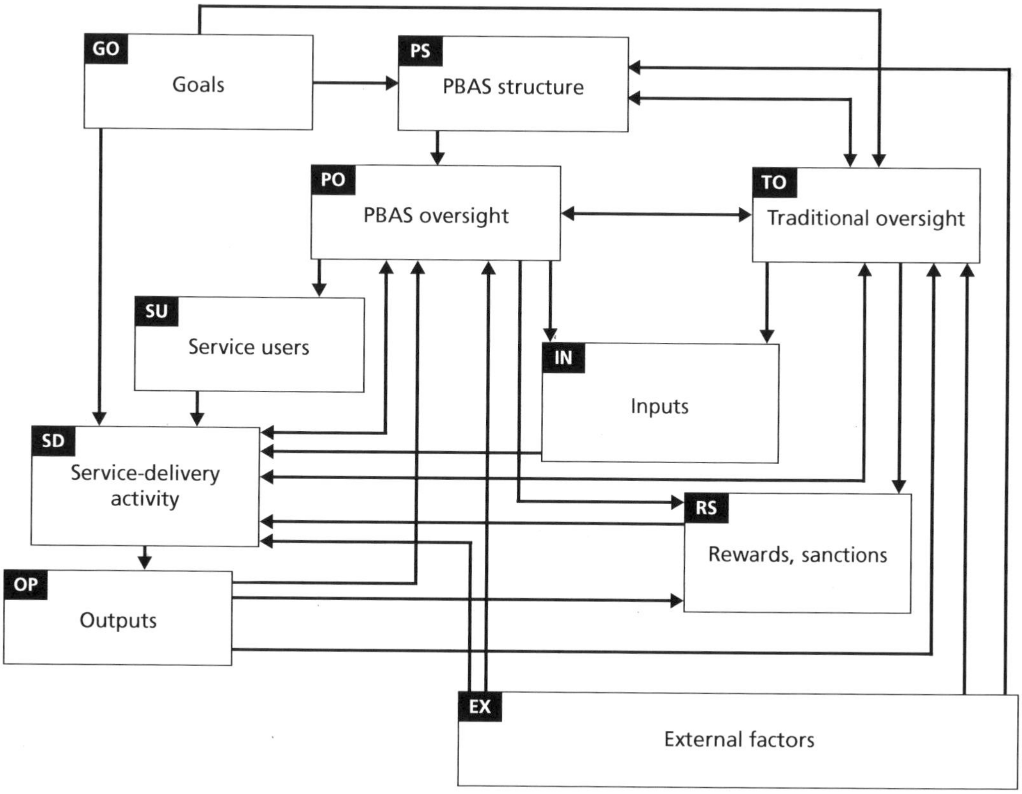

RAND *TR-853-2.4*

this direct oversight responsibility under the PBAS are well aligned with those of the policymakers that created and updated the PBAS, these direct overseers will implement the PBAS as it was intended (box PO). However, there are many reasons that this oversight might not occur as policymakers had envisioned. External factors can require departures from the initial plan for the structure of the PBAS (box EX). And if the PBAS overseers do not share the values of policymakers who created and updated the plan, implementation can depart still further from what planners anticipated. Many years of policy analysis have cautioned us that it takes great energy and discipline to translate high-level policy ideas into concrete programs administered in specific locations. As big ideas migrate down within and across organizations, the local constituencies enlisted to implement them might interpret them differently. Even if they do understand them the same way, implementers might bring local resources and values to bear in ways that change the initiative envisioned above them.[15] In some cases, implementers can seize a new opportunity for change to move the organization in a direction that is more consistent with the values in the local setting, regardless of what high-level leaders prefer.[16]

The new set of goals for the PBAS will also affect the government's approach to traditional administrative oversight activities that continue alongside the PBAS (box TO).

At the beginning of the period of accountability, both PBAS administrative overseers and traditional administrative overseers convey information on the incentive structures to the service-delivery activity (arrows TO->SD and PO->SD). Overseers responsible for the implementation of the PBAS structure (box PO) can work with those responsible for traditional administrative oversight (box TO), including those responsible for delivering resources to the service-delivery activity and those responsible for motivating performance in that activity through traditional communication programs, moral suasion, standard operating procedures and rules, and so on. As before the PBAS, public information about the goals for the activity itself flowing outside the boundaries of the formal PBAS oversight arrangements might provide moral suasion to the service-delivery activity beyond that flowing through formal PBAS administrative oversight channels (via arrow GO->SD). For example, professional standards that teachers absorb from their long association with a school system and their colleagues can potentially encourage them to work hard to improve student learning regardless of formal incentives based on test scores.

In principle, one oversight office could perform both oversight functions; direct PBAS oversight would simply be one part of a well-integrated oversight activity that includes all direct oversight activities. When one integrated office does not exist, the service-delivery activity can easily find itself subject to conflicting goals and oversight. For example, the traditional oversight office might not adjust its rules to give the service-delivery activity discretion to make any improvements that the PBAS oversight office seeks to induce. Alternatively, the traditional oversight office might not change its career-management policies in practice in ways that allow the PBAS to reward good performers and sanction bad performers.

[15] For example, when a customer uses technical services, the provider of those services typically understands more about how the services support the customer than the customer does. When this is true, the customer often allows a technical specialist to define what *performance* means for the customer. It is easy for the technical specialist to emphasize metrics it understands rather than metrics relevant to its customer. It should not be surprising if we observed this occurring as PBASs are implemented.

[16] See, for example, Bardach (1979), W. Williams (1980), and the RAND studies by Paul Berman and Milbrey McLaughlin from the 1970s. Berman and McLaughlin (1975, 1978) and Berman et al. (1977) are illustrative.

Both PBAS overseers and traditional administrative overseers monitor ongoing performance in the service-delivery activity (arrows SD->TO, SD->PO, OP->TO, and OP->PO). As before the PBAS, overseers can respond to what they observe, interacting actively with the service-delivery activity. How the activity runs and the outputs that result will still almost inevitably bring responses from traditional and PBAS direct overseers, tying the decisions of the overseers to the level of performance in the activity during any period of performance.

At the end of the period of accountability, the PBAS and traditional overseers collect the values of metrics relevant to the incentive structure (again, arrows SD->TO, SD->PO, OP->TO, and OP->PO). The information could be quite similar to that collected before the PBAS, but relative emphasis should shift from process metrics to metrics that measure the quantity, quality, and cost of outputs.

The overseers then use the processes defined in the PBAS plan and traditional arrangements to transform information on these metrics into rewards or sanctions for those associated with the service-delivery activity (box RS). Ideally, the PBAS plan and traditional arrangements are tailored so that they complement one another. But this need not be the case. For example, traditional arrangements might dictate exactly what a teacher teaches every day and dictate that the teacher's compensation is based solely on time in service. If those arrangements remain in place, the teacher is limited in his or her ability and motivation to respond to a new PBAS. Nonetheless, even in the absence of any coordination, overseers use the processes defined in the PBAS plan and traditional arrangements to transform information on metrics into rewards or sanctions. These rewards and sanctions can now take one of two forms. The most direct is similar to that described for traditional oversight. It entails changes in budget or roles and responsibilities to a service-delivery activity or changes in monetary compensation, responsibilities, access to training, and so on for individuals (arrows TO->RS and PO->RS).

Alternatively, the overseers can publicize information on the service-delivery activity's level of performance (arrow PO->SU). A PBAS can use this channel when it attempts to change behavior in service-delivery activities with outputs that private-sector users buy. For example, the government might seek to affect behavior in child-care centers or hospitals by collecting and publicizing information about performance in these activities. When a service-delivery activity lies outside the government, all inputs and outputs might also lie outside the government. But the government presumably pursues a PBAS because it cares about specific outcomes that it expects to flow from some service-delivery activity.

Information provided by a PBAS will presumably reward good performers with higher demand and poor performers with lower demand. An increase in demand that increases a firm's salable output (box OP) typically increases the firm's profits, generating an effective reward (arrow OP->RS). Conversely, a reduction in demand that leads to a reduction in salable output reduces the firm's ability to cover fixed costs and so reduces profits, effectively sanctioning the firm.

As noted earlier, a PBAS can be designed to collect information from boxes SD and OP for longer-term evaluation of the PBAS itself through a feedback loop that could allow policymakers to adjust the PBAS plan from one period of accountability to the next.

The Total System

The items and relationships shown in Figures 2.1 through 2.4 are, in fact, subsystems of a larger system comprising a PBAS and the environment in which it operates. Figure 2.5 brings these sets of items and relationships together, all in one place. Here is a very brief overview of the items most important to understanding how a PBAS works and their relationships to one another.

- A service-delivery activity (box SD), such as a school or public health office, transforms inputs (box IN), such as dollars or labor hours, into outputs (box OP), such as high-school graduates or contingency plans for epidemics. These outputs and the way the service-delivery activity produces them can affect long-term outcomes (box OC), such as an educated and healthy citizenry, relevant to policymaker goals (box GO), such as increasing the knowledge and understanding of voters.
- When the service-delivery activity lies inside the government, such as a public school, traditional administrative government oversight (box TO) exists to monitor the service-

Figure 2.5
The Total Analytic Framework for Examining How a Performance-Based Accountability System Works

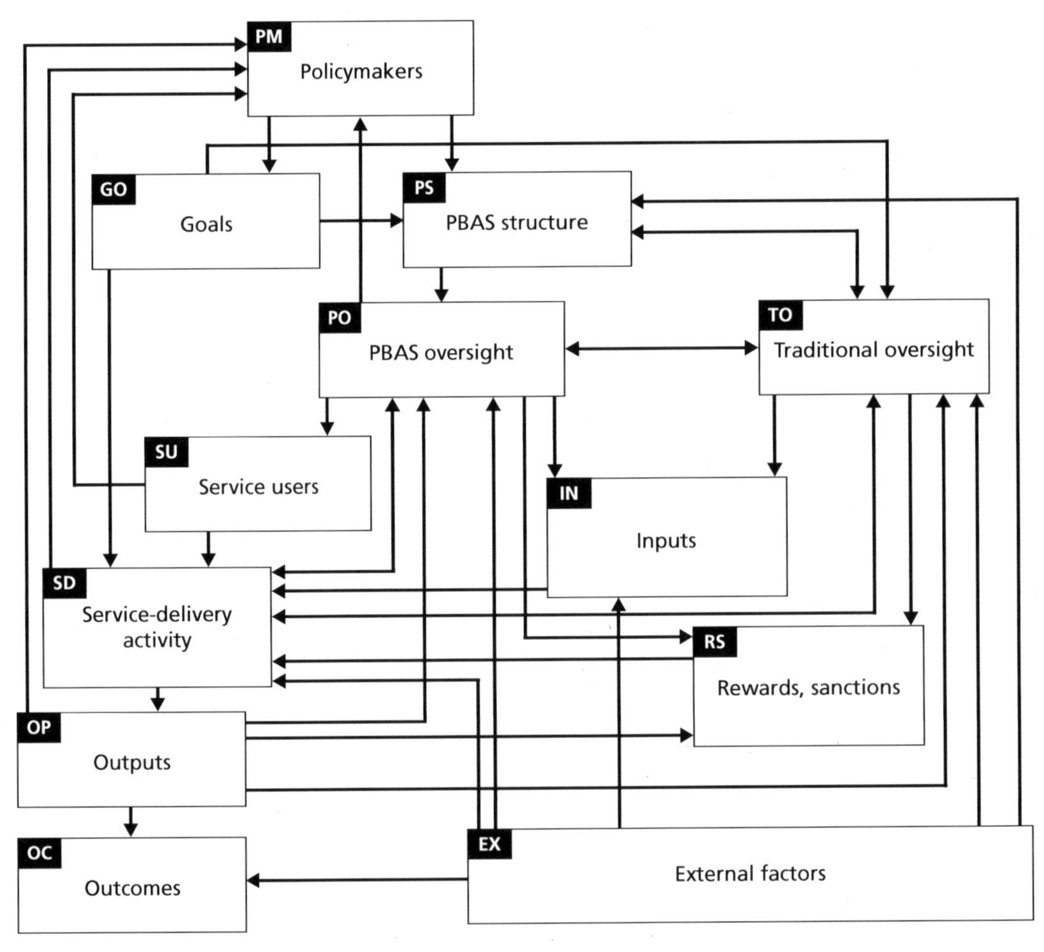

RAND *TR-853-2.5*

delivery activity and shape outcomes through staff reassignment, change in role, and other traditional types of rewards and sanctions about which people in the service-delivery activity care (box RS). When the service-delivery activity lies outside the government, such as a private child-care provider or private hospital, analogous traditional administrative government oversight (box TO) exists to monitor the service-delivery activity and shape outcomes through regulations, taxes, and other traditional types of oversight that yield rewards and sanctions (box RS).

- Users of the service-delivery activity (box SU), such as students or their parents, can affect its output directly by expressing their demands for quality and quantity of output. External factors (box EX)—factors beyond the control of the service-delivery activity or those overseeing it—can shape the ways in which the service-delivery activity's outputs and approach to producing these outputs affect desired outcomes. For example, changes in the demographic community that a public school serves are largely beyond the direct control of the school and its government overseers. They can also shape the effects of overseers' actions to change the behaviors of the service-delivery activity or its employees.
- Under traditional government oversight, various groups might be discontent with outcomes that can be associated with the service-delivery activity. With encouragement from constituents, including those who provide (such as teachers) (box SD) and use (such as students) (box SU) the services delivered, and with information on how the service-delivery activity operates (box SD) and what it produces (box OP), policymakers (box PM) might create (and then repeatedly update) a PBAS to improve outcomes associated with the service-delivery activity. The deliberations of these policymakers yield both high-level goals for outcomes (box GO) and a PBAS structure (box PS).
- In creating their PBAS structure, the policymakers and their planners might consider external factors beyond their control (box EX), and they might seek to integrate the PBAS plan with traditional administrative oversight of the service-delivery activity (box TO). For example, a school district could alter its promotion policies to reflect the incentive structure of a PBAS overseeing school performance in that district. This PBAS plan adds a new set of rules and guidelines in place at the beginning of a period of accountability.
- Over the course of a period of accountability, PBAS overseers implement the PBAS plan (box PO), working side by side with traditional administrative overseers (box TO). The oversight might be integrated, or the two parts might function separately, but, in either case, the oversight plan, including the PBAS plan, is communicated to the service-delivery activity (arrows TO->SD and PO->SD).[17] They monitor performance in this activity and adjust policies through the course of the period in response to what they observe (arrows SD->TO, SD->PO, OP->TO, and OP->PO). For example, they could direct technical assistance to schools with lower attendance rates than planned.
- At the close of the period of accountability, the PBAS overseers collect information on relevant performance metrics (arrows SD->PO and OP->PO) and use the PBAS's incentive structure to transform this information into a decision on rewards or sanctions. When the service-delivery activity occurs inside the government, they convey information on this decision to organizations and individuals associated with the service-delivery activity (box RS via arrow PO->RS). When the service delivery is private, they convey per-

[17] As noted earlier, "side by side" need not imply that the PBAS and traditional administrative overseers work hand in hand. Knowing how well they coordinate their oversight is important to understanding the observed performance of the PBAS.

formance information to users of the service delivered (box SU via arrow PO->SU), who then adjust their level of demand for the service (via arrow SU->SD). The level of demand for the service affects what quantity and quality of outputs the service-delivery activity can justify producing (box SD). Given the costs in the service-delivery activity, the quantity and quality of outputs available for sale determine the activity's level of profit (box RS via arrow OP->RS).

- When the service-delivery activity lies inside the government, decisions on budgets, roles and responsibility, promotions, compensation, and other factors not based on formal performance metrics usually flow from administrative oversight processes beyond the PBAS (box TO via arrow TO->RS). When the service-delivery activity lies outside the government, analogous decisions on regulatory compliance, taxes, and the like similarly flow from administrative oversight processes beyond the PBAS (box TO via arrow TO->RS) Meanwhile, subject to the influences of external factors beyond the control of the government or service-delivery activity, the activity's approach to production and the service outputs and unintended consequences it produces under the influence of the PBAS ultimately affect outcomes relevant to citizens, taxpayers, and policymakers that are hard to link directly to the service-delivery activity (box OC).
- Policymakers (box PM) monitor the operation of the service-delivery activity under the PBAS (arrows SD->PM and OP->PM) and update the PBAS plan to improve the performance of the PBAS from one period of accountability to the next. For example, a state board of education (policymaker) might decide to adopt new achievement tests more aligned with state curriculum standards, which essentially alters the manner in which the PBAS defines *student performance.*
- Organizations and individuals in the service-delivery activity also monitor the immediate consequence of the PBAS for them and use what they learn during each period of accountability (arrow RS->SD) to adjust their responses to the PBAS in future periods of accountability. For example, teachers could assess whether the rewards they received at the end of the period were large enough to justify the level of effort they exerted during the period to achieve those rewards.

The appendix inventories, in a single table, the key items and relationships discussed here.

CHAPTER THREE

Empirical Questions to Ask When Studying a Performance-Based Accountability System

Our project has sought to understand the genesis, design, behavior, and performance of PBASs in five different sectors. We have sought to achieve this understanding by approaching individual PBASs and collecting and interpreting empirical information that was readily available about them. The framework in Chapter Two suggests five sets of basic questions to ask about each PBAS that we examined:

- How did the relevant service-delivery activity work before a PBAS existed?
- Why and how did the PBAS come into existence?
- What does the internal design of the PBAS look like? What is the basis for this design?
- How well does the PBAS work to bring performance in line with goals?
- Given the answers to these questions, what can be done to improve our understanding of the PBAS and so to improve its performance?

This chapter elaborates these questions and, drawing on what we learned about PBASs in the five sectors, clarifies what specific questions we found to be most helpful.

How Did the Relevant Service-Delivery Activity Work Before a Performance-Based Accountability System Existed?

We start our analysis of any PBAS by asking how the service-delivery activity looked before the PBAS existed and then ask how the creation and evolution of the PBAS has changed the service-delivery activity. When thinking about the situation before the PBAS existed, two sets of questions are important.

First, how did the service activity work? The questions that follow arise from the considerations highlighted in Figure 2.1 in Chapter Two. What services did it produce? Who consumed these services? How did it produce these services? What inputs did it consume itself in the production of the service in question? In the course of serving its users, did the activity produce things that had undesirable consequences? What factors beyond its control affected the activity's ability to produce and deliver services? What consequences flowed from what this activity did that might interest government policymakers? As noted earlier, these elements of a production chain are the things that an engineer would associate with a process analysis, an economist would associate with a production function, and an evaluation specialist would associate with a logic model.

Example of a Service-Delivery Activity Before PBAS: Surgical Services

Physicians in a medical practice provide thoracic surgeries. A patient consumes these services on the advice of one or more other physicians. An individual physician typically performs a surgery with the support of an anesthesiologist. A resident might perform a procedure under the close supervision of a more experienced surgeon. The surgeon works with other medical professionals who might be part of the practice or employees of the hospital where the surgery occurs. The hospital, the practice, and other individual doctors might each charge for each service they render, using rules negotiated with the patient's insurance company. Many different kinds of medical errors can occur, only some of them under the surgeon's control. The doctor and hospital might have only limited control over the seriousness of the surgeries they perform or support and the risks associated with them. If a surgery occurs under the Department of Veterans Affairs, the government actually provides the surgery and all the care and services associated with it. Under Medicaid or Medicare, the government pays for the surgery and dictates prices for services. Under private insurance, the government's role is quite limited. But even here, it licenses the hospital, physicians, and other medical professions and approves pharmaceuticals available for their use.

Second, what role did the government play in the provision of this service? The questions that follow address the things highlighted in Figure 2.2 in Chapter Two. Was the service simply subject to the laws that all activities must obey—tax laws, occupational and product safety laws, labor and civil rights laws, environmental laws, and so on? Or did the government play some role specific to the activity? For example, did it license providers or the employees that providers hired? Did it provide inputs directly to the activity? Did it buy services from the activity or pay for the products of the service in some other way—for example, through subsidies to the activity or to the activity's customers, suppliers, or employees? Did the government actually organize and directly manage the activity? Did it apply unique regulations to the activity? Did it collect production or performance data on the activity? If so, how did the government use those data? Understanding how any of these government roles worked before the PBAS arrived is important, because a PBAS can displace many of these and, if it does not displace them, must coordinate its own oversight with such government roles.

Why and How Did the Performance-Based Accountability System Come into Existence?

The creation of a PBAS is a change in the status quo that typically takes considerable effort. It is natural to ask what precipitated this effort, who initiated this effort, how they designed and implemented the PBAS, and how implementation shaped the PBAS. It is also natural to ask how much they knew about how the service activity in question actually worked and how much experience they had with performance measurement and management. These are issues relevant to the considerations highlighted in Figure 2.3 in Chapter Two.

Did some specific large event—for example, an epidemic, disaster, or severe budget shortfall or impasse—reveal unexpected weaknesses in the governance arrangements of the status quo ante? Did success with something like a PBAS in one place motivate people elsewhere to try it? Did some growing body of knowledge, accurate or not, steadily provide evidence that change would be worthwhile, to remove a weakness or to exploit an opportunity?

Whatever the forces that initially suggested the desirability of a PBAS, who actually took the initiative to seek change? For example, did consumers of the product demand change? Did third-party professionals build an analytic case for change and bring this case into the public arena? Or was interest motivated primarily by ideological actors—for example, advocates of some form of "good government" or "the social good"? What stake did the service providers,

Example of the Creation of a PBAS: NCLB

The 1983 publication of *A Nation at Risk* (National Commission on Excellence in Education, 1983) documented the poor performance of U.S. students in English and mathematics. Concerns accelerated in the 1990s in the wake of the disappointing performance of U.S. students on the Trends in International Mathematics and Science Study (TIMSS). The poor performance of urban, minority, and limited-English-proficiency students on state tests and the National Assessment of Educational Progress also caused alarm. This growing body of evidence provided the basis for bipartisan support in Congress to hold schools accountable for the performance of their students in English and mathematics. Many individual states had tried programs like this in the 1990s. NCLB, enacted in 2001, built on this experience to extend a program to the whole nation. But to sustain support for this "national" program, Congress also allowed states to retain the discretion to set their own curriculum standards and performance standards. NCLB required states to adopt well-understood student tests to define program performance. It created potentially tough sanctions for schools that did not achieve their states' target levels of performance.

their employees, the unions of their employees, or their suppliers and business partners have in the creation of a PBAS? How did that stake affect their role in creating or opposing the PBAS? Did political or policy entrepreneurs play an important role in sensing support for change and building a coalition to make change possible?

When it became apparent that serious interest existed to create a PBAS, who actually participated in discussions about its design? How broad was participation in this discussion? What role did government officials already involved with the service activity—as regulators, suppliers, funders, managers, customers, or whatever—play in the creation? How much did these officials adjust their relationships with the service activity to promote the goals of the PBAS? If serious opposition to the PBAS existed, how did this opposition affect its goals and design? How strong a consensus emerged on the goals and likely effects of the PBAS?

How much did those involved in designing the PBAS know about how the service activity in question actually operated? Were they interested in changing specific practices within the service activity, presumably with the expectation that such changes would promote desirable outcomes? Or was their interest based entirely on what the activity delivered, in terms of valued outputs, or unintended effects, or cost? How much experience did they have with measuring performance or using performance measures to improve performance?

What change-management techniques did the parties seeking a PBAS use to implement it? Did they, for example, start with experiments, pilots, or a staged, incremental implementation and build on incremental successes to increase support for the PBAS? Or did they feel compelled to use or prefer rapid implementation to achieve broad, full effects quickly? What analysis did they conduct or consult? What methods did they use to communicate among themselves and with others monitoring the creation of the PBAS? Did they use formal training to prepare people for new roles in the PBAS? Did they rely on third-party specialists to facilitate the change? Did these techniques affect the ultimate goals, design, or performance of the PBAS in demonstrable ways?

What Does the Internal Design of the Performance-Based Accountability System Look Like? What Is the Basis for This Design?

The internal structure of a PBAS can change over time based on experience, but it will, by definition, always have two key elements: an *incentive structure* that it uses to motivate individuals or organizational units to change their behavior, and a set of *performance measures* that it uses to link its incentive structure to the realized performance of these individuals or organiza-

Example of PBAS Incentives and Measures: A+B Construction Contracting

A highway department seeks to reduce the time required to repair a bridge as cost-effectively as possible. To do this, it needs to induce a contractor to complete the work faster while maintaining safety and engineering standards and controlling costs. The highway department does this by holding a competitive selection process in which it states the size of the bonus ("B" in the A+B contract) it will pay the winner for each day it reduces the completion time before some target date. Given this bonus, the selection process chooses the contractor that offers the lowest price ("A" in the A+B contract) to execute the repair. The highway uses as its performance metric actual calendar time to completion, adjusted for things the contractor cannot control, such as weather so severe that the contractor cannot work or delays in interim government inspections required to ensure that engineering standards are met. The source selection and the contractual relationship that result from it constitute a PBAS. Such a PBAS is designed to speed completion of repair, but only in ways that maintain highway department standards and do not cost more to execute than they are worth in terms of the time that they save.

tions. The incentive structure and performance measurement work together to define how a PBAS operates during a period of accountability, as highlighted in Figure 2.4 in Chapter Two. We expect the creators of a PBAS to choose its incentive structure and performance measures simultaneously and to adjust both over time to correct problems. For convenience, we discuss them in sequence, starting with the incentive structure a PBAS uses to motivate behavioral change.

A PBAS targets specific individuals or organizations to change their behavior and chooses incentives that are presumably well suited to affecting that behavior. How does a PBAS execute both of these tasks?

Who within the organization must change to achieve the policymakers' goals? Presumably, a PBAS is created to influence behaviors within the service activity. The PBAS incentives could be targeted at different elements of the service-delivery activity: the organization that owns or directly controls the activity, some element within the activity—a subunit, smaller groups or teams, or individuals, such as managers or employees who execute specific tasks that the designers of the PBAS want to affect directly. When the services are complex and many people are involved, it can be difficult to associate responsibility for outputs with specific units, teams, or individuals. There are limits to the authority of individuals, teams, and even large units within a service provider. Logically, a PBAS should not ask individuals or organizations to change things that they cannot influence. Whom does the PBAS target? How do designers decide? To what extent does this decision depend on how much information designers have about how the service activity works internally?

For any organization or individual the PBAS targets, the designers must then choose an incentive to use. Does the PBAS operate by providing information about the service activity to its customers, with the expectation that the customers will change their consumption patterns and so induce the activity to change what service it provides? Does the PBAS link specific rewards or sanctions to specific things that an organization or individual does? If it uses this approach, what kind of rewards or sanctions does it emphasize? Does it prefer rewards or sanctions? Does it use monetary incentives—say, bonuses or fines or changes in budget levels or market share? Does it reward good performers with recognition and sanction poor performers with shame? Does it link the scope of responsibilities or the degree of flexibility granted to an organization or individual to measured performance? How about opportunities for training, promotion, or attractive employment positions for individuals? How strongly does a PBAS link any of these elements of an incentive structure to performance? How does a PBAS decide what combination of these to use in any situation?

A common concern is that many people working in service activities, particularly in the public sector, are intrinsically motivated and that extrinsic incentive structures, such as those described earlier, could be ineffective or even counterproductive by degrading or even displacing intrinsic motivation (Francois, 2000; Propper and Wilson, 2003). How do PBASs address this concern? A common response to poor performance is to add resources, technical assistance, or training to remove behaviors that lead to poor performance. In some circumstances, such a response can be perceived as rewarding failure. How do PBASs use additional assistance to mitigate sources of poor performance without creating a perception of rewards that might encourage persistent poor performance?

Any incentive structure seeking to link rewards and sanctions to performance must define and measure performance. In the framework we are using, a PBAS can define performance in terms of inputs, processes, or outputs. However, the impetus for adopting PBASs is usually to shift the emphasis of oversight toward outputs and things that are more closely related to desired outcomes. It can use thresholds, multiple categories, or continuous scales to measure performance defined in any particular way. It can benchmark performance across time or across comparable service activities or individuals. When benchmarking, it can "condition" (i.e., adjust) measures of performance to account for external factors beyond the control of the individual or organization that the PBAS seeks to incentivize. It can quantitatively aggregate measures into a single measure before applying incentives or use human judgment to weigh the importance of multiple elements of performance. It can use measures not linked to incentives to check whether incentivized measures induce unintended responses.

How does a PBAS decide what combination of these options to use to define and measure performance? How important is the availability or cost of a measure? How does the institutional context frame choices? How does the structure of the PBAS balance (1) a desire to align a measure with policymakers' priorities with (2) the need to align the measure with factors that any individual or organization can actually influence? How does the structure of the PBAS balance (1) policymakers' desire to change an individual or organization's behavior with (2) that individual or organization's ability to make changes that benefit itself more than the PBAS?

Ultimately, we want to ask what combinations of incentive structures and performance measures work best and are most cost-effective. The discussion in Chapter Two strongly suggests that different combinations are likely to be best in different settings. Knowing that, two questions come to mind. First, can we identify any principles that help us understand why combinations of incentive structures and performance measures vary systematically from one type of PBAS to another? Second, can we identify any empirical information on how incremental changes in elements of the incentive structure or performance measures used in any specific PBAS affect the performance of the PBAS itself? Developing defensible insights of either kind will be difficult. If we can apply some analog for the empirical analysis of institutional choices that persist in competitive private-sector settings, it will likely be easier to develop insights of the first type than of the second.[1]

---

[1] When activities operate in competitive settings where they can easily be displaced, it is reasonable to expect that institutional choices that they make persist only if the choices support the activities' survival. In this setting, it is reasonable to expect that institutional choices that persist are well suited to the environments in which they persist. Masten (2000), for example, surveys the empirical literature on choices in contractual design that persist in such a setting. Camm, Bartis, and Bushman (2008, pp. 3–5) present a set of principles drawn from information of this kind. By analogy, to what extent can

How Well Does the Performance-Based Accountability System Work?

Ultimately, we seek empirical information on the cost-effectiveness of PBASs and factors that affect their cost-effectiveness. The total system of relationships shown in Figure 2.5 in Chapter Two provides the analytic framework for understanding how all aspects of the PBAS work together, in its environment, to transform policymakers' goals into realized outcomes that interest them. Two different approaches are available. The first examines perceptions; the second tries to develop quantitative evaluation accounts and compare cost and benefits. The first is far easier but ultimately less reliable than the second.

Surveys can measure beliefs about the desirability of PBASs and about things that affect their desirability. Many broad surveys are available on the use of performance measurement and performance-based management.[2] Are more targeted and, with luck, more detailed surveys available on the use of PBASs in particular sectors? If so, what do they tell us about how different types of stakeholders perceive different types of PBASs in different settings? To what degree have PBASs realized the goals they set for themselves when initiated? If they have not realized those goals, have they been worth the effort? Do they offer a useful path to cost-effective improvement in the future? Considering all of these questions, do they offer usable lessons learned on the initiation, implementation, and refinement of PBASs?

A more rigorous, challenging—and valuable—analysis would ask for more direct evidence of success. What did it cost, in terms of measurable resources and the focus of key senior policymakers, to initiate and implement a PBAS? How easy has it been for the PBAS to learn from its experience and refine its approach? To date, to what degree has a PBAS changed the behavior of the individuals or organizations that it targeted? Have these behavioral changes had the qualitative effects intended? What effects have these behavioral changes had on measurable valued outputs, unintended effects, and costs? Given prevailing beliefs about how the outputs of a PBAS ultimately affect the outcomes about which policymakers care, what effects

Example of Analyzing the Cost-Effectiveness of a PBAS: Child-Care Services

Child-care PBASs are currently voluntary programs to have third-party evaluators score the level of quality of individual providers who agree to participate and be evaluated. There is little agreement on how to measure the quality of the output that individual child-care providers actually achieve. So these programs observe how providers produce child care and rate the quality of their inputs (e.g., personnel) and methods (e.g., safety of the space where children stay). The cost of running such a PBAS is not well known. Its value can be directly measured mainly in terms of participation rates on the part of providers. High participation rates clearly indicate that it adds enough value to justify the costs of participating. Two kinds of benefits accrue to higher-quality providers and so might motivate their participation. First, they can use their scores to distinguish their services from lower-quality services and so presumably charge more. Second, in some states, the state government directs state payments to child-care centers based on their scores; those with higher scores receive more. Some observers believe that child-care PBASs heighten broader awareness of the importance of high-quality child-care services and might be motivating greater analytic efforts to understand what high-quality child care is and how to produce it. It will be analytically challenging to compare the value of these three potential effects of child-care PBASs with their cost in a way that supports a strong consensus on the net value of the PBASs.

we argue that designs of PBASs that appear to dominate in particular types of settings are well suited—cost-effective—in those settings?

[2] See Abramson and Kamensky (2001); Brudney, Hebert, and Wright (1999); Burgess and Metcalfe (1999); Ferlie (1998); Kettl (1998); Kettl and DeIulio (1995); Lynn (2006); Moon and deLeon (2001); Moynihan (2006); National Academy of Public Administration and Financial Accounting Foundation (1997); Osborne and Gaebler (1993); Poister and Streib (1999); Radin (2003); Sterck (2007); Thompson (2002); and Wang (2002) for selected examples.

has the PBAS had on those outcomes? On net, to date, have its benefits justified its costs? Looking forward, under what circumstances are future benefits likely to exceed future costs?

What Can Be Done to Improve Our Understanding of the Performance-Based Accountability System and to Improve Its Performance?

The questions outlined in the previous section provide a simple framework for organizing and interpreting empirical information available on PBASs in the five sectors that we examine. Gaps in such information point to two kinds of analytic opportunities. First, where information is missing on an individual PBAS, these gaps suggest what information the PBAS or its evaluators can develop to help assess the PBAS's own performance and to help the PBAS refine its design and implementation to improve that performance. Where such information is missing for multiple PBASs and across sectors, these gaps suggest the basis for a broader program of empirical public policy analysis to improve our understanding of how PBASs come into being, how they work in practice, and what factors contribute most to their success in realizing their goals. Our organization of available empirical information in our five sectors ultimately allowed us to identify the potential for developing new information that could be used in either way.

Our analysis revealed a relative dearth of empirical answers to the questions posed in the previous section. That finding naturally pointed to the potential for additional work that could move in either of two directions. The first would seek to identify why so little empirical analysis is available and what can be done to rectify that. Do PBASs simply prefer not to expose themselves to the kind of evaluation that they apply to others? Do they lack the political motivation, analytic capabilities, or resources to evaluate themselves? Could others take on this responsibility if appropriate resources were available?

The second direction would look at remaining questions that empirical analysis might help answer to improve the performance of specific PBASs and to improve our broader understanding about when and how to use PBASs to improve performance. This second direction should lead to the identification of empirical analytic methods best suited to use to improve individual PBASs and to improve our broader application of PBASs. Simpler methods might provide the best support for pilots, incremental implementation, and the refinement of a PBAS.

Example of Long-Term Analysis and Development: PHEP

Performance metrics are under development that could, in the future, be used to measure the quality of state and local PHEP programs—programs that create infrastructure and relationships, develop plans, and train personnel so that public health agencies will be prepared to respond effectively to large-scale emergencies, such as hurricanes, epidemics, and terrorist attacks. In the future, some of these metrics could be used in a PBAS that allocates federal support to such programs, support positively tied to higher performance scores. PHEP metrics that might serve this new role remain immature. Various PHEP programs have developed large suites of performance metrics for as long as the programs have existed, but this is a new application. Among other things, it requires careful attention to standardization to ensure equitable treatment of all governments affected. Ultimately unsuccessful efforts to do something similar to support the allocation of resources among public transit districts illustrate how challenging this will be. The potential exists for PHEP to learn from PBASs from other sectors; the challenge lies in understanding the factors underlying the design of metrics in other settings and then adapting them appropriately for application in the PHEP setting. Opportunities also exist to assess and disarm barriers to developing new PHEP metrics, building evaluation activities into ongoing PHEP programs explicitly designed to support the design of these new metrics, and building the analytic capabilities within PHEP activities to apply the analytic tools most appropriate to the design and assessment of these new metrics, whatever those tools might be.

Potentially very complex methods could be used in longer-term studies seeking to untangle the complexities outlined in Chapter Two and latent in many of the questions listed in this chapter.

CHAPTER FOUR

Conclusions

Interest continues in performance-based public management around the world. So does the paucity of empirical evidence on the actual effects of such management. This report describes the framework we used to organize readily available empirical information on one form of performance-based management—what we refer to as a PBAS. Such a system identifies organizations or individuals who must change their behavior for the performance of an activity to improve, chooses an implicit or explicit incentive structure to motivate these organizations or individuals to change, and then chooses performance measures tailored to inform the incentive structure appropriately. Such systems are pervasive but still maturing.

This report describes how we organized and interpreted readily available empirical information on PBASs in the child-care, education, health-care, PHEP, and transportation sectors, mainly in the United States. We organized this information around questions that fall into five categories:

- How did the relevant service-delivery activity work before a PBAS existed?
- Why and how did the PBAS come into existence?
- What does the internal design of the PBAS look like? What is the basis for this design?
- How well does the PBAS work?
- Given the answers to these questions, what can be done to improve our understanding of the PBAS and so to improve its performance?

Looking forward, analysts could use the questions identified here to seek empirical information in other sectors and other parts of the world. Additional empirical information could help refine existing PBASs and, more broadly, improve decisions on where to initiate new PBASs, how to implement them, and then how to design, manage, and refine them over time.

APPENDIX

Inventory of Key Elements Relevant to How a Performance-Based Accountability System Works

Table A.1 summarizes the elements and relationships described in Chapter Two. The boxes and arrows referenced in the table correspond to the boxes and arrows shown in Figures 2.1 through 2.5 in that chapter. Bracketed numbers 1 through 5 shown in the description of each object of interest refer to the figures in which the text in Chapter Two refers directly to an object of interest.

Table A.1
Key Elements Relevant to How a Performance-Based Accountability System Works

Element	What It Represents
Box PM	Policymakers work together at various levels in what is potentially a multijurisdictional system to create a PBAS. Over time, they work together to adjust the PBAS repeatedly [3, 5].
Arrow PM->GO	Policymakers adjust their high-level goals to govern the PBAS and its relationship with traditional oversight [guidance].
Arrow PM->PS	Policymakers direct creation of a plan for the structure of the PBAS [guidance].
Box GO	Policymakers finalize their high-level goals [2, 3, 4, 5].
Arrow GO->PS	High-level policymaker goals frame their plan for the structure of a PBAS [guidance].
Arrow GO->TO	High-level policymaker goals frame traditional oversight. Introduction of a PBAS can change the goals relevant to traditional oversight or affect how traditional oversight interprets the goals stated in the past [guidance].
Arrow GO->SD	Service-delivery activity is aware of high-level policymaker goals. For a nongovernmental PBAS, the service-delivery activity might be aware of the goals of the PBAS and of high-level government goals. These goals could be conveyed by twin arrows from potentially competing sets of goals [information].
Box PS	Planning for the structure of the PBAS defines how high-level policymakers want it to work over the course of a future period of accountability. Planning covers the definition of performance metrics, measures, incentive structures, and adjustments of traditional government oversight activities, especially the delegation of authority on how to run the service-delivery activity [3, 4, 5].
Arrow PS->TO	Planning for the structure of the PBAS interacts with planning for other elements of government oversight of the service-delivery activity. This complements arrow TO->PS. Arrow PS->TO is likely to be absent for a nongovernmental PBAS [interaction among officials, offices].
Arrow PS->PO	Planners convey the structure of the PBAS to direct overseers. Direct overseers adjust the structure to reflect their own priorities and understanding of the structure [guidance, interpretation of guidance].
Box EX	External factors beyond the control of the government and the service-delivery activity can affect its operation and performance. The government and service-delivery activity can predict the effects of some external factors; some effects are complete surprises to them [1, 2, 3, 4, 5].

Table A.1—Continued

Element	What It Represents
Arrow EX->PS	External factors affect planning for the structure of the PBAS [substantive effects, information].
Arrow EX->TO	External factors affect planning for other elements of government oversight of the service-delivery activity. Direct overseers beyond the PBAS track the status of external factors and use this information to manage the service-delivery activity during the period of accountability [substantive effects, information].
Arrow EX->IN	External factors affect the availability of inputs to be conveyed to the service-delivery activity [substantive effects].
Arrow EX->PO	Direct overseers in the PBAS track the status of external factors and use this information to manage the service-delivery activity during the period of accountability and to calculate rewards and sanctions in explicit incentive structures [information].
Arrow EX->SD	External factors affect the service-delivery activity's ability to produce outputs [substantive effects].
Arrow EX->OC	External factors affect how service outputs are ultimately transformed into outcomes relevant to policymakers [substantive effects].
Box TO	Planning for and execution of elements of government oversight of the service-delivery activity beyond the PBAS. This includes rules and regulations, standard budgeting systems, standard personnel-management and compensation systems, standard operating procedures, cultural and professional norms, and moral suasion [2, 3, 4, 5].
Arrow TO->PS	Planning for other elements of government oversight of the service-delivery activity interacts with planning for the structure of the PBAS. This complements arrow PS->TO [interaction among officials, offices].
Arrow TO->IN	Direct overseers beyond the PBAS decide what inputs to deliver to the service-delivery activity [guidance].
Arrow TO->PO	Direct overseers of the service-delivery activity beyond the PBAS interact with direct overseers within the PBAS. This complements arrow PO->TO. Arrows TO->PO and PO->TO might interact within an integrated government office that implements the PBAS and all other direct government oversight of the service-delivery activity [interaction among officials, offices].
Arrow TO->SD	Direct overseers beyond the PBAS provide policy guidance to the service-delivery activity, including information on the incentive structure that exists beyond the PBAS. This complements the flow of information in arrow SD->TO [guidance].
Arrow TO->RS	Direct overseers beyond the PBAS monitor the service-delivery activity and use their own incentive structures to translate what they observe into rewards and sanctions for decisionmakers within the service-delivery activity [e.g., promotions, compensation, training, future opportunities].
Box IN	Inputs from outside the service-delivery activity can be available for its use [1, 2, 4, 5].
Arrow IN->SD	Inputs are delivered to the service-delivery activity. These include any physical, service, information, or financial resources that the activity might employ with its own assets to produce and deliver its own outputs [substantive resource flows].
Box PO	The PBAS provides for direct oversight of the service-delivery activity [3, 4, 5].
Arrow PO->PM	Policymakers can monitor the processes used by the direct overseers within the PBAS during any period of performance to assess whether they should adjust their guidance in the future [information].
Arrow PO->TO	Direct overseers within the PBAS interact with direct overseers of the service-delivery activity beyond the PBAS. This complements arrow TO->PO. Arrows TO->PO and PO->TO might interact within an integrated government office that implements the PBAS and all other direct government oversight of the service-delivery activity [interaction among officials, offices].
Arrow PO->IN	Direct overseers within the PBAS can potentially direct the delivery of services, such as technical assistance or training related to the PBAS, to the service-delivery activity [guidance].

Table A.1—Continued

Element	What It Represents
Arrow PO->SU	Direct overseers within the PBAS monitor the service-delivery activity and use the PBAS's implicit incentive structure to translate what they observe into performance information provided to users of the output of the service-delivery activity [information].
Arrow PO->SD	Direct overseers within the PBAS provide policy guidance to the service-delivery activity, including information on the PBAS incentive structure. This complements the flow of information in arrow SD->PO [guidance].
Arrow PO->RS	Direct overseers within the PBAS monitor the service-delivery activity and use the PBAS's explicit incentive structure to translate what they observe into rewards and sanctions for decisionmakers within the service-delivery activity. Actual delivery of rewards and sanctions might occur through transitional oversight activities [e.g., promotions, compensation, training, future opportunities].
Box SU	Parties outside the service-delivery activity use its output [2, 3, 4, 5].
Arrow SU->PM	Information from users of the output of the service-delivery activity that is provided to or collected by policymakers. This information might flow through multiple channels, all summarized for simplicity by a single arrow [information].
Arrow SU->SD	Users' expressed demand for the output of the service-delivery activity. When the activity sells its output, this demand helps determine the revenue earned by the service-delivery activity [information, money].
Box SD	The service-delivery activity transforms inputs into outputs in the face of uncertainties and factors beyond its control, under the guidance it receives from direct government overseers inside and outside the PBAS [1, 2, 3, 4, 5].
Arrow SD->PM	Policymakers collect information from within the service-delivery activity or receive it by other means. This information might flow through multiple channels, all summarized for simplicity by a single arrow [information].
Arrow SD->TO	Direct overseers beyond the PBAS collect information on how the service-delivery activity operates. This complements the flow of guidance in arrow TO->SD [information].
Arrow SD->PO	Direct overseers within the PBAS collect information on how the service-delivery activity operates. This complements the flow of guidance in arrow PO->SD [information].
Arrow SD->OP	The service-delivery activity produces output with observable quantity, quality, and cost [substantive resource flows, effects].
Box OP	The output of service-delivery activity can be characterized in terms of its quantity, quality, and cost. This output includes unintended or unanticipated effects [1, 2, 3, 4, 5].
Arrow OP->PM	Policymakers collect information on the output of the service-delivery activity or receive it by other means. This information might flow through multiple channels, all summarized for simplicity by a single arrow [information].
Arrow OP->TO	Direct overseers outside the PBAS collect information on the output of the service-delivery activity [information].
Arrow OP->PO	Direct overseers within the PBAS collect information on the output of the service-delivery activity [information].
Arrow OP->RS	When the service-delivery activity sells its output, the quantity, quality, and costs of output affect the activity's net revenue, directly affecting the rewards or sanctions that it experiences, regardless of government decisions on rewards or sanctions [money].
Arrow OP->OC	Output flows from service-delivery activity ultimately generate outcomes relevant to policymakers that cannot be directly linked to the service-delivery activity [substantive resource flows, effects].
Box RS	Rewards and sanctions accrue over the period of performance for decisionmakers in the service-delivery activity [2, 4, 5].

Table A.1—Continued

Element	What It Represents
Arrow RS->SD	Decisionmakers in the service-delivery activity observe the rewards and sanctions their decisions yield in one period of accountability and use this information to shape their decisions in future periods of accountability [information].
Arrow RS->PO	PBAS overseers monitor the rewards and sanctions that their decisions yield in any period of performance to learn how they should adjust their decisions in the future to achieve the results they desire [information].
Box OC	Outcomes relevant to policymakers accrue but cannot easily be directly linked to the service-delivery activity [1, 5].

Glossary of Related Ways to Improve an Organization's Performance

lean production. A systematic approach to process improvement that (1) identifies all steps in the process used to generate some output, (2) eliminates steps that "add no value" relevant to the output, and (3) increases the value that other steps provide. It was most clearly described from a Western perspective in Womack, Jones, and Roos (1991) and derives from the production system developed at Toyota.

new public management. An approach that seeks to emulate private-sector practices by (1) treating beneficiaries of public programs as customers, (2) highlighting what products these customers want, and (3) using competition among potential sources (public or private) and other innovative forms of motivation to improve how agencies provide the products customers want.

quality-based management. A family of formal methods that (1) clarify what customers want, (2) define all the processes used to provide what customers want, and (3) continuously improve understanding of what customers want and the cost-effectiveness of the processes that provide what customers want. These methods always address cost and effectiveness from a total-system point of view, not that of any individual process.

performance-based accountability system (PBAS). A term we offer for a formal system that improves accountability in a service activity by combining performance measurement in that activity with a well-defined mechanism that rewards good performance or sanctions poor performance in the activity.

performance-based management. Organizational management that is formally informed by performance measures that can potentially help relevant decisionmakers, inside or outside a public- or private-sector organization, to make informed decisions that improve performance in that organization.

performance budgeting. A performance-based accountability system that rewards a government agency that demonstrates good measured performance by increasing its budget and sanctions a government agency that demonstrates poor measured performance by reducing its budget.

performance measurement. Formal use of well-defined qualitative or quantitative, empirically based metrics to track the performance of an activity or organization over time or compare the performance of different activities or organizations at any point in time.

reinventing government. A set of practices described in Osborne and Gaebler (1993) that governments have used to encourage entrepreneurial innovation in government activities at all levels.

Six Sigma. A formal set of tools based on statistical decision theory, first developed and applied at Motorola, that help reduce the variability of outputs in a production process and thereby continuously reduce the defect rate associated with that production process.

Bibliography

Abramson, Mark A., and John M. Kamensky, eds., *Managing for Results 2002*, Lanham, Md.: Rowman and Littlefield Publishers, 2001.

Asch, Beth J., "Do Incentives Matter? The Case of Navy Recruiters," *Industrial and Labor Relations Review*, Vol. 43, No. 3, February 1990, pp. 89S–106S.

Atkinson, A. B., *Atkinson Review: Final Report—Measurement of Government Output and Productivity for the National Accounts*, Basingstoke, UK: Palgrave MacMillan, 2005.

Austin, Robert D., *Measuring and Managing Performance in Organizations*, New York: Dorset House, 1996.

Baker, George, Robert Gibbons, and Kevin J. Murphy, "Subjective Performance Measures in Optimal Incentive Contracts," *Quarterly Journal of Economics*, Vol. 109, No. 4, November 1994, pp. 1125–1156.

Baldwin, Laura H., Frank Camm, and Nancy Y. Moore, *Strategic Sourcing: Measuring and Managing Performance*, Santa Monica, Calif.: RAND Corporation, DB-287-AF, 2000. As of May 19, 2010: http://www.rand.org/pubs/documented_briefings/DB287/

Bardach, Eugene, *The Implementation Game: What Happens After a Bill Becomes a Law*, Cambridge, Mass.: MIT Press, 1979.

Baron, James N., and David M. Kreps, *Strategic Human Resources: Frameworks for General Managers*, New York: John Wiley, 1999.

Behn, R. D., "Why Measure Performance? Different Purposes Require Different Measures," *Public Administration Review*, Vol. 63, No. 5, September 2003, pp. 586–606.

Berman, Paul, and Milbrey Wallin McLaughlin, *Federal Programs Supporting Educational Change*, Vol. IV: *The Findings in Review*, Santa Monica, Calif.: RAND Corporation, R-1589/4-HEW, 1975. As of May 19, 2010: http://www.rand.org/pubs/reports/R1589.4/

———, *Federal Programs Supporting Educational Change*, Vol. VIII: *Implementing and Sustaining Innovations*, Santa Monica, Calif.: RAND Corporation, R-1589/8-HEW, 1978. As of May 19, 2010: http://www.rand.org/pubs/reports/R1589.8/

Berman, Paul, Milbrey Wallin McLaughlin, Gail V. Bass-Golod, Edward Pauly, and Gail L. Zellman, *Federal Programs Supporting Educational Change*, Vol. VII: *Factors Affecting Implementation and Continuation*, Santa Monica, Calif.: RAND Corporation, R-1589/7-HEW, 1977. As of May 19, 2010: http://www.rand.org/pubs/reports/R1589.7/

Booher-Jennings, Jennifer, "Below the Bubble: 'Educational Triage' and the Texas Accountability System," *American Educational Research Journal*, Vol. 42, No. 2, Summer 2005, pp. 231–268.

Brudney, Jeffrey L., F. Ted Hebert, and Deil S. Wright, "Reinventing Government in the American States: Measuring and Explaining Administrative Reform," *Public Administration Review*, Vol. 59, No. 1, 1999, pp. 19–30.

Burgess, Simon, and Paul Metcalfe, *The Use of Incentive Schemes in the Public and Private Sectors: Evidence from British Establishments*, Bristol, UK: Centre for Market and Public Organisation, working paper 00/015, November 1999.

Burgess, Simon, and Marisa Ratto, "The Role of Incentives in the Public Sector: Issues and Evidence," *Oxford Review of Economic Policy*, Vol. 19, No. 2, January 2003, pp. 285–300.

Burke, Brendan F., and Bernadette C. Costello, "The Human Side of Managing for Results," *American Review of Public Administration*, Vol. 35, No. 3, 2005, pp. 270–286.

Burke, John, "Ontario's Municipal Performance Measurement Program: Fostering Innovation and Accountability in Local Government," *Government Finance Review*, Vol. 21, No. 3, June 2005, pp. 22–27.

Camm, Frank, James T. Bartis, and Charles J. Bushman, *Federal Financial Incentives to Induce Early Experience Producing Unconventional Liquid Fuels*, Santa Monica, Calif.: RAND Corporation, TR-586-AF/NETL, 2008. As of May 19, 2010:
http://www.rand.org/pubs/technical_reports/TR586/

Camm, Frank, Cheryl Damberg, Laura Hamilton, Kathleen Mullen, Christopher Nelson, Paul Sorensen, Brian Stecher, Martin Wachs, Allison Yoh, and Gail Zellman, "Improving Performance Based Accountability (PBAS) for Public Services," Santa Monica, Calif.: RAND Corporation, unpublished research.

Carman, Joanne G., "Evaluation Practice Among Community-Based Organizations: Research into the Reality," *American Journal of Evaluation*, Vol. 28, No. 1, 2007, pp. 60–75.

Center on Education Policy, *Answering the Question That Matters Most: Has Student Achievement Increased Since No Child Left Behind?* Washington, D.C., May 31, 2007. As of May 19, 2010:
http://www.cep-dc.org/
index.cfm?fuseaction=document.showDocumentByID&nodeID=1&DocumentID=200

Christensen, Mark, and Peter Skærbæk, "Framing and Overflowing of Public Sector Accountability Innovations: A Comparative Study of Reporting Practices," *Accounting, Auditing and Accountability Journal*, Vol. 20, No. 1, 2007, pp. 101–132.

Condrey, Stephen E., ed., *Handbook of Human Resources Management in Government*, 2nd ed., San Francisco, Calif.: Jossey-Bass, 2005.

Courty, Pascal, and Gerald Marschke, "Making Government Accountable: Lessons from a Federal Job Training Program," *Public Administration Review*, Vol. 67, No. 5, September–October 2007, pp. 904–916.

Cunningham, Gary M., and Jean E. Harris, "Toward a Theory of Performance Reporting to Achieve Public Sector Accountability: A Field Study," *Public Budgeting and Finance*, Vol. 25, No. 2, June 2005, pp. 15–42.

Curristine, Teresa, "Performance and Accountability: Making Government Work," *OECD Observer*, No. 252–253, November 2005, pp. 11–12.

Dixit, Avinash, "Incentives and Organizations in the Public Sector: An Interpretative Review," *Journal of Human Resources*, Vol. 37, No. 4, Autumn 2002, pp. 696–727.

Ellig, Jerry, "Scoring Government Performance Reports," *Public Manager*, Vol. 36, No. 2, Summer 2007, pp. 3–8.

English, Linda M., "Performance Audit of Australian Public Private Partnerships: Legitimising Government Policies or Providing Independent Oversight?" *Financial Accountability and Management*, Vol. 23, No. 3, August 2007, pp. 313–336.

Feller, I., "Performance Measurement Redux," *American Journal of Evaluation*, Vol. 23, No. 4, Winter 2002, pp. 435–452.

Ferlie, Ewan, "The New Public Management in the United Kingdom: Origins, Implementation, and Prospects," paper presented at the International Seminar on Managerial Reform of the State, Brasilia, Brazil, November 1998.

Fernandez, Sergio, "What Works Best When Contracting for Services? An Analysis of Contracting Performance at the Local Level in the US," *Public Administration*, Vol. 85, No. 4, December 2007, pp. 1119–1141.

Folz, D. H., "Service Quality and Benchmarking the Performance of Municipal Services," *Public Administration Review*, Vol. 64, No. 2, March 2004, pp. 209–220.

Francois, Patrick, "'Public Service Motivation' as an Argument for Government Provision," *Journal of Public Economics*, Vol. 78, No. 3, November 2000, pp. 275–299.

Gasper, Des, "Evaluating the 'Logical Framework Approach' Towards Learning-Oriented Development Evaluation," *Public Administration and Development*, Vol. 20, No. 1, February 2000, pp. 17–28.

Gershon, Peter, *Releasing Resources to the Front Line: Independent Review of Public Sector Efficiency*, London: HM Stationery Office, July 2004.

Gormley, William T. Jr., and David Leo Weimer, *Organizational Report Cards*, Cambridge, Mass.: Harvard University Press, 1999.

Halachmi, Arie, "Performance Measurement: Test the Water before You Dive In," *International Review of Administrative Sciences*, Vol. 71, No. 2, 2005, pp. 255–266.

Hamilton, Laura S., "Assessment as a Policy Tool," *Review of Research in Education*, Vol. 27, 2003, pp. 25–68. Reprint available as RP-1163 (2004), as of May 20, 2010:
http://www.rand.org/pubs/reprints/RP1163/

Hamilton, Laura S., Brian M. Stecher, Julie A. Marsh, Jennifer Sloan McCombs, Abby Robyn, Jennifer Russell, Scott Naftel, and Heather Barney, *Standards-Based Accountability Under No Child Left Behind: Experiences of Teachers and Administrators in Three States*, Santa Monica, Calif.: RAND Corporation, MG-589-NSF, 2007. As of May 20, 2010:
http://www.rand.org/pubs/monographs/MG589/

Hatry, Harry P., with Joseph S. Wholey, *Performance Measurement: Getting Results*, Washington, D.C.: Urban Institute, 1999.

Heckman, James, Carolyn Heinrich, and Jeffrey Smith, "Assessing the Performance of Performance Standards in Public Bureaucracies," *American Economic Review*, Vol. 87, No. 2, May 1997, pp. 389–395.

———, "The Performance of Performance Standards," *Journal of Human Resources*, Vol. 37, No. 4, Fall 2002, pp. 778–811.

Heinrich, Carolyn J., "Evidence-Based Policy and Performance Management," *American Review of Public Administration*, Vol. 37, No. 3, September 2007, pp. 255–277.

Hemingway, James, "Sources and Methods for Public Service Productivity: Health," *Economic Trends*, No. 613, December 2004, pp. 82–90. As of May 20, 2010:
http://www.statistics.gov.uk/CCI/article.asp?ID=989

Ho, Alfred Tat-Kei, "Accounting for the Value of Performance Measurement from the Perspective of Midwestern Mayors," *Journal of Public Administration Research and Theory*, Vol. 16, No. 2, April 2006, pp. 217–237.

Jacob, Brian Aaron, *Accountability, Incentives and Behavior: The Impact of High-Stakes Testing in the Chicago Public Schools*, Cambridge, Mass.: National Bureau of Economic Research, working paper 8968, 2002. As of May 20, 2010:
http://papers.nber.org/papers/W8968.pdf

Kahn, Charles M., Emilson C. D. Silva, and James P. Ziliak, "Performance-Based Wages in Tax Collection: The Brazilian Tax Collection Reform and Its Effects," *Economic Journal*, Vol. 111, No. 468, January 2001, pp. 188–205.

Kaplan, Robert S., ed., *Measures for Manufacturing Excellence*, Boston, Mass.: Harvard Business School Press, 1990.

Kelly, Janet M., "Citizen Satisfaction and Administrative Performance Measures: Is There Really a Link?" *Urban Affairs Review*, Vol. 38, No. 6, 2003, pp. 855–866.

Kerr, Steven, "On the Folly of Rewarding A, While Hoping for B," *Academy of Management Journal*, Vol. 18, No. 4, December 1975, pp. 769–783.

Kerr-Perrott, Deirdre, Bryan Shane, and Patricia Lafferty, "Measuring Up: CRA's Materiel Group Systematically Measures Performance," *Summit*, Vol. 8, No. 2, March 2005, pp. 4–6.

Kettl, Donald F., *Reinventing Government: A Fifth-Year Report Card*, Washington, D.C.: Center for Public Management, Brookings Institution, 1998.

Kettl, Donald F., and John J. DiIulio, *Inside the Reinvention Machine: Appraising Governmental Reform*, Washington, D.C.: Brookings Institution, 1995.

Kluvers, Ron, "Program Budgeting and Accountability in Local Government," *Australian Journal of Public Administration*, Vol. 60, No. 2, June 2001, pp. 35–43.

Koretz, Daniel M., "Limitations in the Use of Achievement Tests as Measures of Educators' Productivity," *Journal of Human Resources*, Vol. 37, No. 4, Fall 2002, pp. 752–777.

———, "Attempting to Discern the Effects of the NCLB Accountability Provisions on Learning," paper presented at the Annual Meeting of the American Educational Research Association, Chicago, Ill., 2003.

Koretz, Daniel, and Sheila Barron, *The Validity of Gains in Scores on the Kentucky Instructional Results Information System (KIRIS)*, Santa Monica, Calif.: RAND Corporation, MR-1014-EDU, 1998. As of May 20, 2010:
http://www.rand.org/pubs/monograph_reports/MR1014/

Lazear, Edward P., *Personnel Economics for Managers*, New York: John Wiley, 1998.

———, "Personnel Economics: Past Lessons and Future Directions—Presidential Address to the Society of Labor Economists, San Francisco, May 1, 1998," *Journal of Labor Economics*, Vol. 17, No. 2, April 1999, pp. iv, 199–236.

Levine, Arnold, and Jeffrey Luck, *The New Management Paradigm: A Review of Principles and Practices*, Santa Monica, Calif.: RAND Corporation, MR-458-AF, 1994. As of May 20, 2010:
http://www.rand.org/pubs/monograph_reports/MR458/

Light, Paul Charles, *The Tides of Reform: Making Government Work, 1945–1995*, New Haven, Conn.: Yale University Press, 1997.

Linn, Robert L., "Assessments and Accountability," *Educational Researcher*, Vol. 29, No. 2, 2000, pp. 4–16.

Lonty, Zsuzsanna, and Robert Gregory, "Accountability or Countability? Performance Measurement in the New Zealand Public Service, 1992–2002," *Australian Journal of Public Administration*, Vol. 66, No. 4, December 2007, pp. 468–484.

Lynn, Laurence E. Jr., *Public Management: Old and New*, New York: Routledge, 2006.

Masten, Scott E., "Contractual Choice," in Boudewijn Bouckaert and Gerrit de Geest, eds., *Encyclopedia of Law and Economics*, Vol. III: *The Regulation of Contracts*, Cheltenham, UK: Edward Elgar, 2000, pp. 25–45.

McLaughlin, John A., and Gretchen B. Jordan, "Using Logic Models," in Joseph S. Wholey, Harry P. Hatry, and Kathryn E. Newcomer, eds., *Handbook of Practical Program Evaluation*, 2nd ed., San Francisco, Calif.: Jossey-Bass, 2004, pp. 7–32.

Melkers, Julia, and Katherine Willoughby, "Models of Performance-Measurement Use in Local Governments: Understanding Budgeting, Communication, and Lasting Effects," *Public Administration Review*, Vol. 65, No. 2, March 2005, pp. 180–190.

Martin, Valérie, and Marie-Hélène Jobin, "La gestion axée sur les résultats: Comparaison des cadres de gestion de huit juridictions," *Canadian Public Administration*, Vol. 47, No. 3, September 2004, pp. 304–331.

Micheli, Pietro, Steve Mason, Mike Kennerley, and Mark Wilcox, "Public Sector Performance: Efficiency or Quality?" *Measuring Business Excellence*, Vol. 9, No. 2, 2005, pp. 68–73.

Moon, M. Jae, and Peter deLeon, "Municipal Reinvention: Managerial Values and Diffusion Among Municipalities," *Journal of Public Administration Research and Theory*, Vol. 11, No. 3, 2001, pp. 327–351.

Morley, Elaine, Scott P. Bryant, and Harry P. Hatry, with Joseph P. Wholey, *Comparative Performance Measurement*, Washington, D.C.: Urban Institute, 2001.

Moynihan, Donald P., "Managing for Results in State Government: Evaluating a Decade of Reform," *Public Administration Review*, Vol. 66, No. 1, January–February 2006, pp. 77–89.

Moynihan, Donald P., and Patricia Wallace Ingraham, "Look for the Silver Lining: When Performance-Based Accountability Systems Work," *Journal of Public Administration Research and Theory*, Vol. 13, No. 4, 2003, pp. 469–490.

———, "Integrative Leadership in the Public Sector: A Model of Performance-Information Use," *Administration and Society*, Vol. 36, No. 4, 2004, pp. 427–453.

National Academy of Public Administration, *Questions and Answers for Improving Government Performance: Operationalizing Performance Management*, Washington, D.C., paper 99-07, 1999.

———, *Questions and Answers for Improving Government Performance: Designing Effective Performance Measures*, Washington, D.C., paper 99-08, 1999.

National Academy of Public Administration and Financial Accounting Foundation, Governmental Accounting Standards Board, *Report on Survey of State and Local Government Use and Reporting of Performance Measures: First Questionnaire Results*, 1997.

National Commission on Excellence in Education, *A Nation at Risk: The Imperative for Educational Reform—A Report to the Nation and the Secretary of Education, United States Department of Education*, Washington, D.C., 1983. As of May 21, 2010:
http://purl.access.gpo.gov/GPO/LPS3244

National Statistics, "Improvements in Measuring Health Service Productivity," news release, London, February 27, 2006. As of May 20, 2010:
http://www.ons.gov.uk/about-statistics/ukcemga/publications-home/press-releases/public-service-productivity--health.pdf

Osborne, David, and Ted Gaebler, *Reinventing Government: How the Entrepreneurial Spirit Is Transforming the Public Sector*, New York: Plume, 1993.

Page, Stephen, "Measuring Accountability for Results in Interagency Collaboratives," *Public Administration Review*, Vol. 64, No. 5, September 2004, pp. 591–606.

Perrin, Burt, "Performance Measurement: Does the Reality Match the Rhetoric? A Rejoinder to Bernstein and Winston," *American Journal of Evaluation*, Vol. 20, No. 1, 1999, pp. 101–111.

Poister, Theodore H., and Robert P. McGowan, "The Use of Management Tools in Municipal Government: A National Survey," *Public Administration Review*, Vol. 44, No. 3, May–June 1984, pp. 215–223.

Poister, Theodore H., and Gregory Streib, "Performance Measurement in Municipal Government: Assessing the State of the Practice," *Public Administration Review*, Vol. 59, No. 4, July–August 1999, pp. 325–335.

Propper, Carol, and Deborah Wilson, "The Use and Usefulness of Performance Measures in the Public Sector," *Oxford Review of Economic Policy*, Vol. 19, No. 2, Summer 2003, pp. 250–267.

Public Law 103-62, Government Performance and Results Act of 1993, August 3, 1993.

Public Law 107-110, No Child Left Behind Act of 2001, January 8, 2002.

Radin, Beryl A., "Intergovernmental Relationships and the Federal Performance Movement," *Publius: The Journal of Federalism*, Vol. 30, Nos. 1–2, Winter–Spring 2000, pp. 143–158.

———, "A Comparative Approach to Performance Management: Contrasting the Experience of Australia, New Zealand, and the United States," *International Journal of Public Administration*, Vol. 26, No. 12, January 2003, pp. 1355–1376.

Rowan, Brian, "Standards as Incentives for Instructional Reform," in Susan Fuhrman and Jennifer A. O'Day, eds., *Rewards and Reform: Creating Educational Incentives That Work*, San Francisco, Calif.: Jossey-Bass, 1996, pp. 195–225.

Siverbo, Sven, and Tobias Johansson, "Relative Performance Evaluation in Swedish Local Government," *Financial Accountability and Management*, Vol. 22, No. 3, August 2006, pp. 271–290.

Stecher, B. M., "Consequences of Large-Scale, High-Stakes Testing on School and Classroom Practice," in Laura S. Hamilton, Brian M. Stecher, and Stephen P. Klein, eds., *Making Sense of Test-Based Accountability in Education*, Santa Monica, Calif.: RAND Corporation, MR-1554-EDU, 2002, pp. 79–100. As of May 20, 2010:
http://www.rand.org/pubs/monograph_reports/MR1554/

Stecher, Brian, Frank Camm, Cheryl Damberg, Laura Hamilton, Kathleen Mullen, Christopher Nelson, Paul Sorensen, Martin Wachs, Allison Yoh, and Gail Zellman, *Toward a Culture of Consequences: Performance-Based Accountability in Public Services*, Santa Monica, Calif.: RAND Corporation, MG-1019, 2010. As of August 2010:
http://www.rand.org/pubs/monographs/MG1019/

Sterck, Miekatrien, "The Impact of Performance Budgeting on the Role of the Legislature: A Four-Country Study," *International Review of Administrative Sciences*, Vol. 73, No. 2, June 2007, pp. 189–203.

Thompson, Frank J., "Reinvention in the States: Ripple or Tide?" *Public Administration Review*, Vol. 62, No. 3, May–June 2002, pp. 362–367.

Thompson, F. J., and L. R. Jones, *Reinventing the Pentagon: How the New Public Management Can Bring Institutional Renewal*, San Francisco, Calif.: Jossey-Bass, 1994.

van Dooren, Wouter, "What Makes Organisations Measure? Hypotheses on the Causes and Conditions for Performance Measurement," *Financial Accountability and Management*, Vol. 21, No. 3, August 2005, pp. 363–383.

van Helden, G. Jan, and Sandra Tillema, "In Search of a Benchmarking Theory for the Public Sector," *Financial Accountability and Management*, Vol. 21, No. 3, August 2005, pp. 337–361.

Wang, Xiaohu, "Assessing Administrative Accountability: Results from a National Survey," *American Review of Public Administration*, Vol. 32, No. 3, 2002, pp. 350–370.

Weil, David, Archon Fung, Mary Graham, and Elena Fagotto, "The Effectiveness of Regulatory Disclosure Policies," *Journal of Policy Analysis and Management*, Vol. 25, No. 1, Winter 2006, pp. 155–181.

Whittaker, James B., *Balanced Scorecard in the Federal Government*, Vienna, Va.: Management Concepts, 2001.

Williams, D. W., "Measuring Government in the Early Twentieth Century," *Public Administration Review*, Vol. 63, No. 6, November 2003, pp. 643–659.

Williams, Walter, *The Implementation Perspective: A Guide for Managing Social Service Delivery Programs*, Berkeley, Calif.: University of California Press, 1980.

Womack, James P., Daniel T. Jones, and Daniel Roos, *The Machine That Changed the World: How Japan's Secret Weapon in the Global Auto Wars Will Revolutionize Western Industry*, New York: HarperPerennial, 1991.

Wynn-Williams, K. L. H., "Performance Assessment and Benchmarking in the Public Sector: An Example from New Zealand," *Benchmarking*, Vol. 12, No. 5, 2005, pp. 482–492.